THE SENSE OF
PLACE

Fritz Steele

THE SENSE
OF PLACE

CBI Publishing Company, Inc.
51 Sleeper Street
Boston, Massachusetts 02210

CBI

Production Editor: Becky Handler
Text Designer: Margaret Ong Tsao
Compositor: TKM Productions

ACKNOWLEDGMENTS

The following excerpts are reprinted by permission:

What Time Is This Place?, by Kevin Lynch, pp. 57, 62–63, 80, 178, 196, reprinted by permission of MIT Press, copyright © 1972 by The Massachusetts Institute of Technology.

The Man Who Walked Through Time, by Colin Fletcher, pp. 5–6, 22–23, 43, 120, 197, reprinted by permission of Alfred A. Knopf, copyright © 1968.

Robert Benchley: A Biography, by Nathaniel Benchley, pp. 184–188, reprinted by permission of International Creative Management, copyright © 1955 by Nathaniel Benchley.

All photographs are by the author except as noted in photograph captions.

ISBN 0-8436-0135-3

Printed in the United States of America

Printing (*last digit*): 9 8 7 6 5 4 3 2 1

To my daughter, Lauren Steele

Contents

Preface

What makes an experience in one setting particularly exciting or satisfying, while the experience in an apparently similar setting turns out to be dull or distasteful? How much do we know about a particular spot from having been there for one specific purpose at one time of the day, week, or year? How do some people do such an impressive job of creating a personal place that says volumes about themselves, while others can live for long periods in a house and impose practically no traces of personality?

Questions about place phenomena such as these have long held a strong fascination for me, and this book is the result of much time spent trying to explore the function of place experiences in our lives. In the process I have been able to enjoy two aspects that I find particularly interesting: getting to know new settings quickly, and practicing ways to know familiar settings better.

One point should be made clear at the outset: this book is not about places per se, but about our *sense* of place, the way it affects our lives, and the ways in which we create our own. One of the main themes is the difference between settings, physical and social, and the sense of place that is our experience of them, heavily influenced by our own contributions. We therefore cannot know what a place is like in a vacuum, independent of the people who will experience it.

This book is thus not really about psychology, or about design of environments, but about the interaction between features of settings and features of the people who use them, with a particular look at the choices we make as users and how they affect our sense of place. At the least I would hope that the discussion helps reduce our tendency to lay all the responsibility for our place experiences onto the setting, and to be blind to our own contributions, good or bad. I also do not intend the book simply to be a dump on the typically bland, nonspirited settings being created today—plenty of writers have already done that. What I have tried to provide is some better dimensions for expanding our own awareness of high quality place experiences and how to help them to happen in even relatively limited settings. The desired end would be to be able to describe the richness of our place reactions rather than just summing them up in global ways as "great" or "lousy."

This book is not about all people everywhere. If I had attempted to write such a book, I suspect that it would have ended up being of value to no people anywhere. It is, in fact, heavily influenced by my own personal experiences in the United States and the United Kingdom; and therefore people who live in those or similar cultures will find it easiest to identify with my examples and conclusions. I have tried, however, to draw out the human patterns behind the specific examples, so as to suggest the possibility of some consistent processes at work in different cultures.

My intended audience is not professionals in environmental psychology, but rather people who must live, work, and play someplace, and who could therefore profit from a better understanding of the ways in which they relate to their settings. The book is also not intended necessarily for an urban audience, although I suppose that the majority of readers will live in or near urban areas. Many of them, however, will spend their time in a variety of settings, and I have used examples from a range that spans city, suburb, country, and wilderness.

There is one specialized segment of readers who I particularly hope will become interested in the ideas and themes here: those who are in a position to make decisions that have a significant impact on the settings of other people. They would include planners and designers, members of town councils, environmental planning groups in communities, preservation trust members, managers of facilities in work organizations.

Because this discussion is not really aimed at just the academic community, I have tried to remain aware of the primary mission of communicating to readers in a manner that is lively and related to their immediate experiences. To this end, I have drawn upon a variety of sources and types of examples including photographs and written quotations. The written materials include biographical examples, my own personal experiences, fictional accounts of place experiences, and research results where appropriate.

Finally, many people have helped me in developing the themes and ideas for this book, both directly and others through example. Some of the most direct supporters included Deborah Jones-Steele, David Sellers, Patrick Taylor,

Michele Metraux, and Leonard Zweig. I would also like to thank the people at Walber's on the Delaware for creating such a good setting for writing, and everyone at Master Color Service in Boston for their unending support with the photographs.

THE SENSE OF
PLACE

PART ONE

SETTINGS, PLACE, AND EXPERIENCE

1   A Feel for
Place Experiences

Imagine several people wandering along the sidewalk in New York's Fifth Avenue shopping district on a busy spring weekday. What kind of place is it for them? That is an impossible question to answer without knowing more about them and how they came to be there. Let us assume they include a visitor from a small town in Kansas, a confirmed city-lover who has spent her whole life in New York City, a businessman who has just suffered a major setback, and a sneak thief who thrives in jostling crowds. Each would experience a personal sense of place on that busy sidewalk, each stimulated by different feelings, threats, and opportunities.

The things they would be aware of would also vary considerably: the thief would see the mass of people as a mix of clients, ground cover, and potential pursuers; the businessman would wonder why all these successful people showed up on this particular day to flaunt their good fortune in front of him; the native New Yorker would be particularly taken with the variety of displays in the shop windows, and how several of them have been changed to create a spring mood; and the Kansas resident would be excited about the people and shops, puzzled about where a moderately priced lunch counter could be found on Fifth Avenue, and vaguely uneasy about not being able to see very far ahead, and certainly not to the horizon.

What kind of place is this?
It depends on whom you
ask. . . .

The point of this scenario should be clear: experience of place on the Fifth
Avenue sidewalk can never really be described as simply a function of its physical attributes; we must also take into account the eyes, ears, intentions, and
moods of the persons who are experiencing it. It is not a place, in a vacuum: it
is a *setting* in which people may experience a sense of place, given the right
conditions.

This book is written with the intention of stimulating readers to make
greater sense of the place experiences they have had and will have in the future. I believe that in the United States we tend to grow up with relatively confused and conflicting notions about place experiences, and to develop a poor
understanding of the nature of settings and how to use them well without destroying them in the process. I also believe that we tend to be relatively unaware of *choices* we make about where we do things and how we do them,
without making the connection between choices and place experiences.

When people are unaware or unappreciative of the ways in which place
experiences affect their lives, for better or worse, the places tend not to have
much conscious influence on the nature of the experiences. People seem to be
willing to overlook a poor setting (or accept "inferior goods") in ways they
would not if they were making decisions about an automobile or a new outfit,
possibly because the costs of a poor setting are more subtle and less conspicu-
ous than those of a malfunctioning car or a badly fitting suit. Yet the actual
human costs to us of bad place experiences can be enormous when accumulated over a lifetime.

SETTINGS, PLACE, AND EXPERIENCE

An example of inferior place goods. Who are these benches built for? Shadows and fumes are their main attributes, and so far no one seems to use them at all.

Let me put this view of the impact of place experiences into historical perspective for a moment. "Place" may be one of the most frequently used words in the English language. It is used variously as a physical location (what places did you visit?), a psychological state (I'm not in a very good place right now), social status (people should know their place), the location of something in one's mind (I can't quite place it), a standard for evaluation (there's a time and place for everything), and on and on. The meanings of the word have been as varied (and often as confused) as the ingenious human mind could make them.

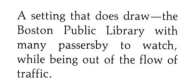

A setting that does draw—the Boston Public Library with many passersby to watch, while being out of the flow of traffic.

This richness is not accidental; it reflects the large role that place has played throughout human history. It has been a significant factor in people's day-to-day experiences, whether they were coping with the dangers around their caves in pre-Roman Britain, or with noise and pollution around their Chicago apartments in 1980. People have identified themselves with places, called them home, and used them to provide symbolic identities that distinguish themselves from anybody else. People have also identified others by the places they come from, and often attributed characteristics to them based on this identification. ("He's a New Yorker, Southerner, Californian, Greek, Scot, and so on—and you know what *they're* like!")

This strong identification with places has often taken on a larger meaning than just home. Certain places became symbols of power, principles, and ideals, and consequently were rallying points for wars, conquests, and other dramatic historic events. Rome, Carthage, Peking, Mecca, and Jerusalem were much more than just geographic sites: they have stood for abstract concepts for which people would fight and die.

Places have shaped human history in other, less dramatic, ways as well. People who lived in a particular location tended to take their visible setting as the total world, and to develop a cosmology or world view shaped by that location. Cultures that developed on islands or coasts had the sea as a major active force in their mythic history, while Indians in America's southwest emphasized the relationship between the earth and the sky, their two most dominant place features.

Attitudes toward places have grown out of these views, but they have also changed over time as cultures changed. The Europeans' view of mountains, for instance, shifted in the nineteenth century from the traditional one of awe, romanticism, and curiosity, to one of nonchalance and acceptance as the developing technology of travel made mountains more accessible and less dangerous to explore. Individual attitudes have been important, as places have been blamed or given credit for people's experiences: "New York was a lousy place," or "the place was very depressing," "Paris was so exciting," or "New England was breathtaking in the autumn." As my opening scenario has already suggested, whether one blames or praises a particular spot often has as much to do with what one brings to it as it does with the attributes of the setting itself.

People have avoided places that they believed to be dangerous or proscribed: Death Valley, haunted houses, sacred burial grounds, and the Gobi Desert, to name a few. They have also sought out places that they believed to be particularly desirable or auspicious: the Fountain of Youth, El Dorado, Mount Olympus, Lourdes, Atlantis, and so on. A quality that has spurred both seeking and avoidance is sacredness: the investment of a place with religious significance, which is a special symbolic power. People have also been drawn to places that are either well known and thus familiar, or unknown and mysterious, and therefore appealing to curiosity. I would guess that the advent of films and television has drastically reduced this spirit of mystery, as so much more information is now available about formerly inaccessible locations.

Places have shaped the characters of their residents, as in the differences between a taciturn, slow-to-warm Vermonter and an outgoing, talkative Arizonan. In the reverse direction, people have reshaped the character of a location over time, often creating entirely new settings. Los Angeles in 1980 is a very different setting than it was in 1880; they are literally worlds apart. People have also adapted themselves to places they could not or chose not to change. This often takes the form of deadening or blocking awareness in order to control consistently bad place experiences. For example, homeowners living near a pungent pig farm would rely less on sense of smell for their place satisfactions, and would thus smell fewer of those smells they used to enjoy, as the price for reducing the pig presence in their lives.

One of the most consistently important contributions of place has been to provide a sense of security to individuals and groups: a feeling that they are at home or have a home that they can go back to, which provides a sense of control over their own fate. Whether or not this has a good effect depends on how extreme it becomes; however, security can become limiting by making people unwilling to venture out and risk the uncertainties (and potential stimulation) of new experiences.

Security in a setting: the clear boundary for a small London residential square.

(Courtesy of the British Tourist Authority)

At the present time, there seems to be a steady trend in the industrialized nations toward characterless settings that have no special personality or distinguishing spirit. In the United States, the pattern of housing developments, fast-food establishments, and gas stations has tended to wipe out regional differences in architecture and building materials. The only thing that keeps parts of Seattle, Washington from looking exactly like Route 1 in Saugus, Massachusetts is the looming presence of Mount Rainier (when Seattle's weather is clear enough to allow it to be seen), which developers have not yet figured out how to standardize or obliterate.

In many instances, modern society is tending to destroy the rich variety of places, replacing them with homogenized "efficient" settings that have no variety, surprise, or traces of their own history and development. They may indeed be efficient for certain tasks (such as crossing a city by expressway in a matter of minutes, or providing a choice of five types of hamburger), but they offer minimal returns compared with the traditional impact of places as providers of many levels of meaning and experience.

Because of this drift toward bland, less stimulating settings, the need for improved consciousness of place is greater than it has ever been. We are faced with the conflicting trends of dwindling physical resources and expanding uses and needs for materials in modern society. Our mobility has steadily increased, but because of economic and social constraints our actual options about where and how to live may have begun to shrink. I believe that we need to understand the human place experience much better in order to cope with this squeeze. We need to create richer settings and use existing ones more effectively, and generally to improve their contributions to our lives.

A fairly new setting that encourages rich use and sense of place: Filene's Park in Boston's Downtown Crossing shopping district.

SETTINGS, PLACE, AND EXPERIENCE

It is possible that the rapidly developing enthusiasm for exploration of "inner space" and consciousness-raising techniques is in part a result of dissatisfaction with place ("outer space") experiences in modern American life. Whether or not this is true, we can still apply consciousness raising to spatial awareness and sense of place as well as to sense of self.

MAJOR THEMES

The subject of place is potentially enormous, as all human action and experience occurs in some place of context. I have tried to focus on selected key areas that will help readers obtain a manageable view of their sense of place, without in the process losing the richness of living. With this in mind, the concept of place has been used as both an *object* of people's interest, concern, influence, attention, alteration, and enjoyment, and as a *cause* of people's feelings, moods, responses, constraints, achievements, survival, and pleasure. Both of these approaches are valid, as people and their environments form what are called "transactional systems," with each giving and receiving something from the other.

The sizes or levels of settings that we will be concerned with will be varied, ranging from a personal area such as one's bed or room, through homes, neighborhoods, towns, and geographic regions with a particular character. The scale of setting will vary, because in practice we concern ourselves with different aspects depending on our location, needs, interests, and particular activities of the moment. For instance, when taking a bath the nature of the specific bathroom and its fittings will usually be more relevant to us than the fact that our house is green and located in a hilly area. When trying to leave this same home after a heavy snowstorm, the hilliness of the area is our prime concern, and the nature of the bathroom is no longer relevant.

Talking about a transactional view of relations with the environment is general and abstract. Therefore it may be useful to preview briefly some of the main themes that follow.

- The relationship between people and environment is transactional: people take something (positive or negative) from and give or do things to the environment; these acts may alter the environment's influence on the people.
- I now believe that the concept of place should actually be psychological or interactional, not just physical. The environment is made up of a combination of physical and social features; the sense of place is an experience created by the setting combined with what a person brings to it. In other words, to some degree we create our own places, they do not exist independent of us.
- There are, however, certain settings that have such a strong "spirit of place" that they will tend to have a similar impact on many different people. The Grand Canyon or the left bank of the Seine in Paris are excellent examples.
- Settings obviously have an impact on people, both short-term and long-term, and there are some patterns to this impact.
- People have an impact through how they care for, create new social forces, and design new physical features for settings. This can be positive or negative, short-term or long-term.

The focus here is on patterns of place experience, not on abstract theories or single events out of context. It is my hope that reading this book will stimulate the reader to bring a new curiosity to places. This could be shown by regularly asking diagnostic questions about one's place experiences, such as: What kind of mood is this setting stimulating in me? What are the messages that this particular place holds about what happened here in the past? Can I get more out of this setting by changing the way I'm using it? Am I allowing myself really to experience what this setting has to offer? Can I change the setting in some positive way? Do I want to stay here, or should I move on?

It may seem that I am harping on these types of questions, but I think that one really needs to establish the habit of curiosity about the sense of place in order to enrich it.

2 Settings and the Sense of Place

Although the words place and setting have generally been used interchangeably to refer to a person's immediate location and physical surroundings, I have become convinced that they should be distinguished from one another so that we can better understand their effects on our experiences.

Thus I have tried to be reasonably consistent in using the following terms. "Place" has two aspects: The *sense of place*, which is the particular experience of a person in a particular setting, (feeling stimulated, excited, joyous, expansive, and so forth); and the *spirit of place*, which is the combination of characteristics that gives some locations a special "feel" or personality (such as a spirit of mystery or of identity with a person or group). "Setting" will refer to a person's immediate surroundings, including both physical and social elements.

THE SENSE OF PLACE

A sense of place is the pattern of reactions that a setting stimulates for a person. These reactions are a product of both features of the setting and aspects the person brings to it:

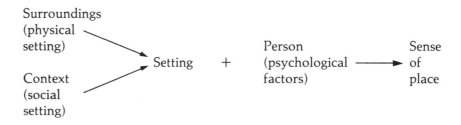

This is obviously a simplification, and there are many complicating factors that will be explored as more specific topics later. The main point here is that sense of place is an interactional concept: a person comes into contact with a setting, which produces reactions. These include feelings, perceptions, behaviors, and outcomes associated with one's being in that location. Sense of place is not limited just to the experiences of which the person is consciously aware; it includes unnoticed influences, such as a consistent avoidance of doing certain things in that particular place.[1]

There are several main types of place experiences I have found to be both frequent and interesting in trying to understand the sense of place (these will be discussed in some detail in Parts IV and V):

- Immediate feelings and thoughts
- Views of the world
- Occupational experiences
- Intimate knowledge of one spot
- Memories and fantasies
- Recognition or newness
- Personal identification with someone's "spot"
- Sense of accomplishment or blockage caused by the setting
- Sense of enjoyment, fun, or displeasure

The emphasis is obviously on our experiences as users of a setting, so that it is hard to talk about a sense of place until we know both about what place and what people we are talking. The setting itself is obviously important, but settings and people mix in different ways, with different (and sometimes unpredictable) results. A suburban shopping mall that is the height of excitement and efficiency to one buyer is a necessary evil to another who recalls arguments that took place in that (or a similar) mall in the past. Both of these are real senses of place, and neither is more true than the other.

A mix of physical and social settings: the large, enclosed shopping mall, which provides variety and control of environment at the same time.

SPIRIT OF PLACE

I do not want to hold too rigidly to the idea that all place experiences are primarily products of a particular time and person. We all know that there are certain physical and social settings that are so potent that they evoke similar responses, regardless of the diversity of internal states of the responders. These settings have what we call a strong spirit of place that acts in a powerful, predictable manner on everybody who encounters them. This magic, with which certain locations seem to be endowed, is certainly a force worth considering.

Examples include:

- Special physical features
- Spirit of people
- Spirit of mystery
- City diseases of the spirit
- Spirit of personal place

DESCRIBING SETTINGS

As I have used the term "settings" many times already, we should not leave these introductory chapters before describing the nature of settings more specifically.

Put most simply, settings are the external environment surrounding a person at a particular location and time. They are made up of both physical and social features that combine to provide forces acting on the person. One clear analogy is a theatrical stage set, in which the physical parts (stage floor, backdrops, lighting, distance from the audience, props) and the social features (roles, scripts, relations among the cast members, expectations and reactions of the audience) combine to influence the behavior and experiences of both actors and audience.

Physical Features

When we refer to the immediate environment we usually mean our physical surroundings. For instance, wherever you are reading these lines at this moment, you are located somewhere that has many features that could potentially influence you: spaces, furniture, fixtures, patterns and intensity of light, sounds, air of a particular temperature, colors and color patterns, other people nearby, and so on.

The physical elements in this Boston setting include the shops, the sidewalk, the passersby, and the "regulars" who gather to talk things over on the sidewalks.

The list of physical elements is potentially long, even for simple settings; thus we usually select certain features as worth perceiving because they somehow affect our activities or feelings while we are there. For instance, some locations have features that make it easy to do a messy task like mixing paint: floors that are easily cleaned, good places to store materials, furniture that is rough, a location that is not visited by a lot of people, no signs telling users not to litter, open spaces, and so on. Other settings would constrain this kind of task: small spaces, easily damaged floors, tables, and walls, or poor lighting.

Physical features affect feelings as well as activities. For example, warm colors (reds, oranges, yellows) have a stimulating effect on mood, while cool colors (greens, blues, greys) generally have a calming or action-reducing impact. These are general tendencies, of course, and do not hold true for all people, or for any one person all the time. In addition, which effect is "better" depends on what one wants to have happen in a particular setting. Other features that consistently affect feelings include textures of walls, floors, and furnishings; levels of natural and artificial lighting; air temperature and humidity; and items that tend to have symbolic significance in a particular culture, such as gates, fences, or locks as symbols of security, or original paintings as symbols of wealth and power.

Social Features

The social context of a setting is the collection of forces that operate on an individual as a result of relationships to other people and social institutions. Although these forces are usually not visible as physical features, their potential numbers can be long and varied. Some examples are: group and institutional norms about acceptable behavior in a particular location, and friendship and hostility patterns that make people more or less likely to want to have contact with or be observed by one another.

Although physical surroundings are clearly important in providing a sense of place, it is easy to overplay their influence and to miss the impact of the social context. For example, a study of walking patterns in an art museum found that both components of the setting were important. Those who knew a study was being conducted were there physically, but they were also aware of being there in a social context as a "member of an experiment, trying to be a good museum-goer and please the experimenters." Thus the physical influence on walking patterns was based partly on layout and items in the museum, while the social influence was shown by the differences in behavior (quicker movement, spreading their attention more equally among the paintings) of those who knew they were part of the study compared with those who did not.[2]

The social context also helps to determine the impact of the physical setting. A golf club locker room containing a sign with a long list of club rules will usually have a different impact on members (who, because of their position as insiders, know how to distinguish between the enforced and unenforced rules), and nonmembers (who feel that there seems to be almost no behavior that is actually allowable). In business organizations, the nature of

(Photograph by Bob Messing)

A setting with its users implied even though absent at this moment: the porch overlooking the golf course at a small New England resort hotel.

administrative rules often determines whether a new building feels like an exciting improvement in one's work life, or a more constraining, brittle setting that cannot be tinkered with in any way without a great deal of effort or potential risk of punishment.

This influence is complicated by the fact that most people are members of several overlapping social systems (e.g., family, friends, profession/business, neighborhood, ethnic group), and may therefore be subject to conflicting pressures about what to do in a given physical setting. Children in innovative school buildings are often caught between teachers' expectations that they be "experimental" with their space and parents' rules about polite public behavior that are often based on the parents' school experiences in a very different setting.

SETTINGS, PLACE, AND EXPERIENCE

The physical setting also affects the impact of the social setting, rendering certain forces more or less potent. Novelist P. G. Wodehouse found that the wide social network of friends and acquaintances in which he and his wife moved exerted a more disruptive influence on his work when they lived in London, where their accessible location made social demands too difficult to avoid:

Dear Bill,

We have taken this house for a year, though I never expect to stay a year in any one spot these days. How is your cottage working out? One thing about living in the country is that, even if the roof leaks, you can get some writing done. I find it's the hardest job to get at the stuff here, as we have so many lunches and dinners which just eat up the time. If I have a lunch hanging over me, it kills my morning's work, and dinner isn't much better. I hate the social life. My dream would be to live in the country with a typewriter and plenty of paper and tobacco and be cut by the county.

(P. G. Wodehouse, *Author! Author!*)

Changing his home's location to some remote country village would not have changed much in how his friends felt about him, but it would certainly have changed how they acted, which would have taken him and his wife out of the day-to-day network of reciprocal entertaining. A London couple's decision to visit would have been a major undertaking rather than an easy way to kill a few hours. In this case, my sympathies are definitely with Wodehouse and his dream of being ignored in the country.

The Complementary Impact of Social and Physical Features

When we want to create a setting that has a certain spirit or satisfies our needs in a particular way, we usually have a range of choices about how to do this: altering the physical features or social system norms, or some combination.

For example, E. T. Hall points out that the need for personal privacy tends to be met differently by Americans and English.

When the American wants to be alone he goes into a room and shuts the door—he depends on architectural features for screening. For an American to refuse to talk to someone else present in the same room, to give them the "silent treatment," is the ultimate form of rejection, and a sure sign of great displeasure. The English, on the other hand, lacking rooms of their own since childhood, never developed the practice of using space as a refuge from others. They have in effect internalized a set of barriers, which they erect and which others are supposed to recognize. Therefore, the more the Englishman shuts himself off when he is with an American the more likely the American is to break in to assure himself that all is well. Tension lasts until the two get to know each other. The important point is that the spatial and architectural needs of each are not the same at all.

(E. T. Hall, *The Hidden Dimension*)

An ever-present feature of airport settings was a response to a social setting problem: the security checkpoint.

Their needs for privacy, however, may be quite similar—they just satisfy those needs in different ways. One uses physical barriers, the other uses social norms through a behavioral signal such as holding a newspaper. Each of these approaches is equally legitimate, and which one will be better in a given instance should depend on physical resources and the ease or difficulty of making the social signals work.

In the earlier example concerning a good physical setting for doing messy tasks, the emphasis was on wall, floor, and surface materials that would not become too messy. A social, and probably cheaper, solution to this problem would be to change the group's norms about what is acceptable wear and tear versus what is messy, so things would not have to be kept that neat. Families who own vacation houses often find that changing their standards of house cleaning is a more economical (and relaxed) solution than trying to re-create their tidy city home environment in a setting of dirt roads, beaches, and outdoor activities.

Having made a great fuss about the distinction between our place experiences and their settings, I would like to restate the main themes of the book. My intention is to show how we often create our own sense of place by what we bring to a setting and how we use it. This also suggests that most places are only settings until there are users there to complete the picture. We can design settings (physical and social), and do it better or worse depending on how well we know the characteristics of likely users, and what values we use to make choices about the experiences that "should" happen there. This is a major dilemma in many newly built environments today, and it is basically a political issue as to whose standards of quality are used in the planning of public buildings, city squares, national park facilities, and the like. We can also do better or worse at using our settings and extracting the varieties of place experiences they potentially provide to us.

NOTES

1. For another recent book that focuses in a different and interesting manner on human experience as the guide to understanding place, see Yi-Fu Tuan, *Space and Place: The Perspective of Experience* (Minneapolis: University of Minnesota Press, 1977).
2. Robert Bechtel, "Human Movement and Architecture," *Transaction*, May 1967, pp. 53–56.

PART TWO

PERSONAL PROCESSES: WHAT PEOPLE BRING TO THEIR SETTINGS

3 Perception and Awareness: What Is This Setting?

Because a sense of place is the result of interplay between a person and a setting, an important determinant of that sense is the means of connecting the two. This connection process can be roughly divided into two general parts: (1) perceiving what is there in the setting and organizing it into usable categories of information, and (2) becoming aware of particular features or combinations of features in a setting at a particular moment.

In this chapter we will consider some basic aspects of the human experiences of perception and awareness. My purpose is not to go into the kind of detail that would be contained in a book on the psychology of perception, but simply to provide a basis for discussing the more central ideas regarding our own roles in experiencing a sense of place.[1]

PERCEPTION: CREATING OUR OWN SCENARIOS

Perception is an information-receiving process wherein a person (1) receives a signal from the immediate setting (sees a bird fly by, smells an oil slick, hears another person utter a sound); and (2) organizes these incoming signals in such a way as to give them meaning within a personal view of the world (identifies the moving object as a "bird" or "seagull," registers the smell as oily, decodes the other person's sounds as speech and understands its meaning, and so on).

In playing its linking function, perception helps us organize external information so that we can feel that we "know" something about what surrounds us and what is likely to happen to us. Having this information provides us with some control over our own fate, so that we are not always at the whim of unpredictable events. The importance of this sense of control is brought home to us when we lose it, as in the experience of diving into murky water where sights and sounds are suddenly cut off.

A second major function of human perception is to deal with the fact that there is always too much to tune into. In almost any setting at any time there are more potential signals than we can receive or process. We are not only limited in the amount of information we can process; we also need to retain some energy (and attention) for activities other than perception. A major problem is how to select what to receive and what to screen out. In relatively safe situations the quality of our decisions may not make much difference. In others, such as passing through a dangerous jungle area, the ability to focus on subtle cues (the rustle of a leaf, a flash of movement ahead) can mean the difference between living and dying. People naturally acquire selection patterns that work best for them in the settings in which the patterns were developed: a resident of the Amazon jungle can perceive the reflection from a snake's skin that would be "invisible" to most New Yorkers; and a New Yorker may be able to hear the "inaudible" sounds of a mugger's crepe soles tip-toeing along a Central Park bicycle path.

This view of perception as a selective process helps to illuminate what was meant in Chapter 2 about persons helping to create their own sense of place. There are many signals in any given setting, but which ones we pick up and how we interpret them shape how we actually experience both the setting and ourselves in it.

A writer named Serge Boutourline has described the difference between an "object-oriented" and "signal-oriented" view of the environment.[2] The object-oriented view says that people are surrounded by articles that have specific properties; the person's ability to perceive the environment is measured by the ability to tune into these properties and use them. The signal-oriented approach says that the environment is made up of an infinite number of signals being sent out by the objects (and lack of objects) surrounding a person. Perception is thus determined by the points on the person's "envelope of space" that receive these signals, and in what order they are received. This theory suggests the analogy of the cinema: we are like directors putting together movie scenarios (our own experiences), using sets and props (our surroundings, including various aids such as other people, transport vehicles, communications devices, drugs) that help us to collect and order signals in some quantity and sequence (the editing process), which then becomes our perception of the "world." We usually think of this experience as simply a function of what's "out there," downplaying our own role in the creation of the scenario.

PERSONAL PROCESSES: WHAT PEOPLE BRING TO THEIR SETTINGS

This view is consistent with the theme of this book, which is that much of our experience of place is determined by how we perceive, organize, and react to signals from our settings, rather than any objective qualities of the settings themselves. Perception is therefore an active contributor to shaping our world, rather than a passive receiver of whatever is around us.

PERCEPTUAL STYLES

The preceding comments have referred to the general process of human perception that is shared by most people. There are also specific styles of perceiving that vary from person to person and group to group. The particular locale and culture in which one is raised will favor some views of the world and discourage others. For example, people who grow up in the United States plains states are more aware of the horizon than those who grow up in city settings where one usually only can see for short distances.

The degree of contrast among parts of our regular settings can determine what we are able to see, as well as our preferences and what we consider to be "beautiful." People who grow up in the Barrens area of the North American Arctic can see the beauty that eludes those who are familiar with more "upholstered" or lush settings.

> Staring out over the limitless brown expanse I at first saw only a rolling world of faded brown, shot through with streaks and whorls of yellow-greens, for when I tried to see it all, the individual colors merged into anonymity. It *was* a barren sight, and yet that desert face concealed a beauty that rose from a thousand sources, under the white sun. The deep chocolate bogs, laden with rich sepia dyes that stain the streams and pools, were bounded by wide swales of emerald sedges and tall grass. On the sweeping slopes that rose above these verdant meadows, the dark and glossy greens of dwarf birch scrub formed amorphous patches of somber vitality that were illuminated by broad spaces where the brilliance of ten million minute flowers drew themselves small butterflies as gorgeous as any in the world.
>
> (Farley Mowat, *People of the Deer*)

While as a visitor it took Mowat some time to see the variations and the beauty in the Barrens, natives of this area would quite naturally see these features, having spent their lives making such distinctions.

Another factor that attunes our perceptual style is our pattern of personal interests. For example, when college president John Coleman took a sabbatical to work as a manual laborer laying sewer lines, he started seeing waste systems that had been invisible to him before. When visiting an art museum on his days off, instead of speculating about the place of art in the world's history, he wondered who had laid the museum's underground pipes.[3] Thus we tend to notice those items that interest us—they become the main figures that we pick out of the larger number of potential signals, and the rest are left as background.

The kind of detail that has considerable variety if you look for it: the suburban fireplug.

PHYSICAL PROPERTIES AND
PERCEPTION

Of course, not all factors that shape a person's particular pattern of perception are qualities of the person. There are some features of physical setting that have been found to have consistent effects on perception. For one, our view of the sizes of objects is influenced by the overall scale of the setting in relation to ourselves. We overestimate sizes when we are small, as is shown in William Saroyan's views of Sunday church services as a child:

> When I sat upstairs to listen to Reverend Knadjian's sermon and looked down at the benches, every place taken, I imagined that there were a great many people there, a multitude, in short. The fact is that the church could scarcely contain two hundred people. The balcony ran around the auditorium. There were two rows of benches on the sides, and four at the back of the balcony. Still, I had always imagined that a great multitude was inside the Church.

> (William Saroyan, *Places Where I've Done Time*)

This relative perception also explains why we can go back to the settings of our childhood, but we can never go back to our childhood places, which were experiences that were mixtures of ourselves and those settings. The large woods we explored are revealed to the adult as a patch of trees in a vacant lot, the kitchen that seemed so formidably vast as Mother's domain now looks tiny and cramped, and so on.

Another important physical property is the degree of closure in a structure. We see spaces as "things" as long as any closure at all provides a boundary that defines an area and gives us something to work with. Nan Fairbrother described this in her wonderful discussion of landscape design for human enjoyment:

Human vision seems naturally inclined to create enclosures in space even when the actual physical barriers are extremely slight, and given the merest suggestion of enclosure we ourselves supply the rest. A widely spaced row of lamp standards, for instance, arched over a road creates a continuous tunnel in space; half a dozen bollards will close off the side of a square for the eye as well as the motor car.

(Nan Fairbrother, *The Nature of Landscape Design*)

People who understand this can create a strong spirit of place for a modest house and front yard simply by placing a few stones, posts, or pieces of fence in strategic spots. Later we will return to the sense of place that can be enriched by contrast, scale, and enclosure, especially when we open ourselves to perceiving settings in new ways.

AWARENESS OF SETTINGS

As noted earlier, perception is only one-half of the process of linking a person to a setting. After perception comes awareness, where the person uses incoming information as raw material for thoughts and feelings about the setting. Awareness can be about specific elements in the setting (colors, floors, walls, trees, odors, and so on), or about patterns and relationships among elements such as distances, relative locations, or contrasting textures.

What Stimulates our Awareness?

Sights Most people are probably familiar with the ways in which the things they see shape their awareness of their setting. That which is seen is partly determined by elements that stand out as "figures," and those that remain in the background; this relationship can be reversed, as when we suddenly become aware of a single detail in a room. In order to see a range of possible sights in a setting, however, we must allow what exists to come into our awareness. People often do the opposite, which is to say, they shape their perception of the setting based on what they are accustomed to seeing or *expect* to see. This habit leads to what the Gestalt psychologists call staring, rather than seeing. Edwin Way Teale observed two experienced starers on the breathtaking crest of the Continental Divide in Colorado's Rocky Mountains:

As we stood discussing such things (as the joy of such a spot), two business men struck up an acquaintance nearby. They talked endlessly, loudly, always on the same subject: the clubs they had belonged to, how one had presided over a grand conclave, how the other had headed a committee that brought in twenty-two new members. All the while the great spiritual experience of the mountains was passing them by. Unseen, unfelt, unappreciated, the beauty of the land unfolded around them. The clubs of the world formed their world entire. It enclosed them like the home of a snail wherever they went. For them, the scene would have been just as moving if they had been hemmed in by billboards.

(Edwin Way Teale, *Journey into Summer*)

One wonders why the men were there to begin with; they were probably "doing" the Rocky Mountains in a day or two.

Not only businessmen have trouble with staring, of course. For many years, explorers who visited the inner gorge of the Grand Canyon in Arizona saw a barren environment because they had been told that the gorge had no plant life except at one area called Vasey's Paradise. This has recently been shown to be quite false; there are many plants that grow in the Canyon, and the barrenness was mostly in the eyes of the beholders.[4]

Because people tend to see in settings what they expect to be there, they often fail to be aware of beauty in unconventional sites that are not labeled "beautiful" by prevailing values. Seeing beauty along the banks of the Seine in Paris fits with what one is supposed to see there; but seeing beauty in the run-down dockside areas of the Thames in London requires one really to look at what is there, and to allow the special patterns of light, texture, reflection, and contrast to be seen for their own beauty, in spite of the fact that many of the elements are old, broken, or derelict.

Three building ends that can be seen as dilapidation or beautiful abstract forms, depending on your point of view.

PERSONAL PROCESSES: WHAT PEOPLE BRING TO THEIR SETTINGS

There is an interesting problem in the English language with the way we describe awareness: we use almost entirely *visual* terms, such as "seeing," and "looking," to give our sense of place awareness. In fact, western European civilizations do rely on sight to the detriment of the other senses, but not as greatly as our vocabulary would suggest.

Smells For impact on our awareness of settings, smells are at least a close second to sights. For instance, farmers generally sense the changing seasons of the year first through changing smells, not through visual cues. Each season has its own distinctive smells, but so do the transition periods, so that a "country smells calendar" would have many more than four recurring seasons on it.

> What a world of the nose the country can be from the cidery smell of apples rotting in the brown, frosty grass under a wild apple tree to the honorable aroma of freshly dug onions spread on sacking in the autumn sun. There are plenty of others, hearty enough, some of them, but all, somehow or other, fit into a country world.
>
> (Henry Beston, *Northern Farm*)

Smells are also an important part of city awareness, but with different patterns. The changes of seasons produce fewer new odors because they are masked by activities such as vehicle traffic and its exhaust fumes that are continuous throughout the year. The variations in smell are sensed from section to section of a city, such as the gamey smells of a market area on a warm day, or tarry smells of soft streets. Cities as a whole may also have characteristic smells: there is a certain whiff of diesel exhaust fumes that always means "London" to me as they are belched throughout the city by the taxis and buses; while New Haven, Connecticut's odors often seem for some reason to remind me of vegetable soup.

A very special corner that *looks* like nothing. Your nose tells you that you're next to a spice company.

Given such patterns, it was inevitable that there would be attempts to design settings with smells to make people more or less aware of setting. In the United States, consumer products companies spend millions in advertising ("Oh, you had fish for dinner? Ughh.") to convince Americans that they should cover all traces of their home life (cooking smells, furniture odors, and so forth) with some anonymous scent such as "green trees," which had nothing to do with activities in the house. In the opposite direction, Vita Sackville-West and Harold Nicolson reportedly designed the gardens at Sissinghurst Castle in Kent to use smells to enhance immediate awareness of the setting. They did this by using mixtures of plantings that provided a succession of fragrances throughout the year, and by planning the relative locations of plants with different scents, so that visitors experienced special fragrance sequences as well as visual sequences while walking through the gardens.[5]

Sounds Although we may notice a particular sound if it is unusual, such as a siren suddenly screaming in the night, our basic reception is made up of a mixture of sounds of different sources, intensities, and degrees of pleasantness (a learned taste except at extremely high, painful levels) that are received more or less together and create an overall "auditory atmosphere." Two settings can have different atmospheres, as Coleman describes so nicely:

> It suddenly hit me today how very noisy the kitchen [of the Union Oyster House Restaurant in Boston] is. The world I am used to [the President's office] at Haverford is such a quiet one. In my office, the only sounds through the day are the IBM typwriter next door, the loud gong of the grandfather clock each hour, the periodic ring of the telephone outside followed by my secretary's warm hello, and whatever quiet conversation there is within. In the Oyster House kitchen, it's a different world entirely. Muzak is constantly playing above my head, with music from my generation or from Broadway hit shows of one or two decades ago. One of the cooks has his radio going still louder, tuned to sports broadcasts, soul music, or what seems like an hourly replay of the hit of the day, "Killing Me Softly." In the busy hours, there is a steady shout of orders, and a reshout of lost orders; and there is the constant flow of social banter. Cooler and range doors bang, frying pans drop, and the steamer lets off steam. And over it all, there is the clatter of china and glassware being sorted into trays and the shoosh and swoosh of water in the dish machines. I know I am where the action is.

> (John Coleman, *Blue-Collar Journal*)

While visual cues on the average make us think verbally of what we see, both smells and sounds have their greatest impact subliminally, that is, not necessarily on the consciousness. A certain smell can change our mood, and the pattern of sounds can affect our mood or our view of the setting without our thinking about it. This was illustrated by an incident in a company whose building was redesigned as an "office landscape," complete with plants and a so-called "white noise generator" to produce an ambient noise level (gentle hum) that would mask conversations and provide privacy. One day the white noise generator broke down, and complaints about the temperature in the office area immediately began. Later discussions showed that the workers had unconsciously associated the hum of the generator with air conditioning noise, which it did, in fact, resemble. When the noise stopped, the office staff made the assumption that the air conditioning had gone off, so therefore it must be getting warmer in the office.

Heightened Awareness

There are certain times when one's awareness of settings suddenly increases dramatically. An example is the situation in which a decision is required, such as a driver arriving at a major junction or crossroad and having quickly to scan the nearby surroundings (buildings, signs, natural features) for cues as to the correct route. This is one reason why the distance seems longer when one is going to a destination for the first time than it does when making the return trip, especially when driving in an automobile. When trying to find the destination initially, one is aware of more elements of the route while looking for potential guide posts and points at which one might be required to make a decision. More details are carefully observed, therefore, and more experience packed into the first trip, making the return trip seem shorter by comparison.

Awareness of our immediate surroundings is also heightened by strangeness. Being "out of our element" often makes us notice features that can be seen (but are seldom noticed) in our home territories; this can open up new possibilities or pleasures within our surroundings. The striking cleanliness of certain European cities tends to jog American tourists' vision so that they notice details such as porches, stoops, steps, and fences that are invisible (but often just as interesting) elements in their own home towns.

Last, changes in body state can lead to greater awareness of surroundings. The most familiar instance is the one when we feel physically ill. At such times we become more sensitive to subtle cues in the setting: currents of moving air, slight sounds, small changes in temperature, hardness of surfaces, increases in light intensity, and so on. At such times we have less energy and attention to devote to simple adaptations to environmental variations that are, in fact, happening all the time, but that are usually screened out of our awareness. Instead, we are more attuned to our body and its relationship to the immediate surroundings. The old-fashioned hangover is a classic case of heightened settings awareness.

My purpose with these points has not been to tout constant awareness of settings, but to show that there are identifiable factors that enhance this sensitivity, and to suggest that to some degree it can be personally controlled. For example, you can make the conscious choice to look for certain features, which generally leads to seeing many new qualities that had previously gone unnoticed. A sculptor friend once started me looking at tin roofs of Vermont barns, and I saw varieties of style, construction, and beauty that had always been there but that had been invisible to me before. Similarly, if you were especially to look at the doorway of every building you entered over the course of a chosen week, you would never again take doorways for granted or be oblivious to their different qualities.

AWARENESS THROUGH CERTIFICATION

In closing this chapter, I want to touch on a special process that can increase awareness of settings in modern urban areas. This process, called "certification," results in a person feeling that his or her setting is somehow special, legitimate, or more real, as it has been certified by some reliable outside source.

As far as I know, the process of certification was first described by American novelist Walker Percy.[6] He suggested that when one sees one's own neighborhood in a movie that personal setting has been authorized as a real someplace, not just anyplace. This serves as an antidote to the modern urban trend toward undifferentiated settings that encourage alienation and disconnection from one's immediate surroundings. Through certification, the person is helped to see them as having distinctive features and a spirit of place.

When certification is considered this way, it can obviously happen in other ways besides seeing one's familiar territories in a commercial film. A similar effect occurs when someone sees the home area on a television news program, or reads about it in a newspaper, magazine, or book. In a study of Parisians' views of their city's special spots, Stanley Milgram found that they accent those international symbols (such as the *Arc de Triomphe*) that have been repeatedly certified by schools and public officials.[7] These choices are to some extent arbitrary social definitions, as they are in any city's school system, but they still shape citizens' views of the "important" locales in their cities.

City locations are often certified by being major stops in the transport system (Boston's Park St. subway station).

PERSONAL PROCESSES: WHAT PEOPLE BRING TO THEIR SETTINGS

My last example has been with us for many hundreds of years: it is the impact of visual arts. To take a modern instance, Cezanne changed the way many people saw the countrysides he painted, as did the other Impressionists and Post-Impressionists. Even today, many visitors to Paris see it less for itself and more as a confirmation of the Paris they "know" through painting. The Ash Can School of painters in New York helped people to see beauty in the mundane underside of a large city's life. In a sense, the rough settings were certified as having value because people were bothering to do paintings of them without cleaning them up or idealizing them.

NOTES

1. For readers who would like more information on human perception, I would recommend J. J. Gibson, *The Senses Considered as Perceptual Systems* (Boston: Houghton Mifflin Co., 1966); the section on "Basic Psychological Processes and The Environment," in H. Proshansky, W. Ittelson, and L. Rivlin (eds.), *Environmental Psychology* (revised ed.) (New York: Holt, Rinehart and Winston, 1976); and Chapters 3 and 4 of David Canter, *The Psychology of Place* (London: The Architectural Press, 1977).

2. Serge Boutourline, "Notes on 'Object-oriented' and 'Signal-oriented' Approaches to the Definition of the Physical World Which Surrounds Individual Human Beings," unpublished paper prepared for Department of Architecture, University of Washington, 1969.

3. John R. Coleman, *Blue-Collar Journal: A College President's Sabbatical*, Philadelphia: J. B. Lippincott, 1974, p. 51.

4. Virginia McConnell Simmons, "Vasey's Paradise Lost?" *National Parks and Conservation Magazine*, Vol. 50, No. 10, 1976.

5. Ann Scott-James, *The Making of Sissinghurst*, London: Michael Joseph Publishers, 1973.

6. Walker Percy, *The Moviegoer*, New York: Alfred A. Knopf, 1961.

7. Stanley Milgram with Denise Jodelet, "Psychological Maps of Paris," in H. Proshansky, W. Ittelson, and L. Rivlin (eds.), *Environmental Psychology* (revised ed.).

4   Our Own Baggage: Expectations, Intentions, and Moods

When people come to a setting, they usually do not arrive empty-handed, open to whatever turns up there. They almost always bring a good deal of "baggage" with them that influences how they perceive, use, and feel about the setting. There are two main psychological factors that shape these reactions: the expectations and intentions about what can be seen and should be done in the setting; and mood that provides a general sense of atmosphere, that indicates whether the surroundings are friendly or hostile—or something in between.

EXPECTATIONS AND INTENTIONS

As was discussed in Chapter 2, the world is so full of potential information and stimulation that it would be totally overwhelming if we brought to it no structure or way of selecting what to notice and what to ignore. One of these structuring devices is our conception of who we are and what we are doing in a particular setting: our intentions for being there, our expectations as to what we and others should or are likely to do there, and our assumptions about the setting itself. We generally allow familiar things to take precedence over unfamiliar ones, because we already have expectations about how the former can be used. For example, someone just arrived from China will first want to see Chinese writing/architecture as familiars, before accomodating to U.S. glass modern and pizza parlors. Another example is a person's judgment as to whether there is "something to do" in a setting (as in, "this town has nothing to do . . . "). That judgment is always rooted in assumptions about what is "worthwhile" or "fun," and can be changed as we break out of our old definitions of what "something" is. New features seem to emerge when we relax our notions about what might be there, and allow what is actually there to be seen.

There are regular expectations that certain symbolic elements set off in us; a flashing red light usually implies danger, and a city curbstone tells us that there is a separate zone for pedestrians where it is safe to walk. We build up our store of expectations for particular features based on a lifetime of experiences, although we have usually long forgotten the original models that set these expectations for us. These features can be any common element of settings: doors, windows, chairs, colors, particular plants or flowers, and so on. We may have such strong expectations for a given setting that we just pass through it without seeing it, as when we walk through our living room without noticing a new vase of flowers, or when we "do" several art galleries or museums in one day.

Is this gate a symbol of security, danger, or nothing? It depends on whether you are the owner, someone being chased, or a passerby.

PERSONAL PROCESSES: WHAT PEOPLE BRING TO THEIR SETTINGS

The art museum often triggers very routine expectations and behaviors that have little to do with the particular setting.

We should bear in mind, however, that the same element may set a different expectation in two different people: one person's oak door as symbol of solidity and status is another's oak door connoting separation and rejection. The same element may also have different meanings in different cultures, so that a Cadillac parked in the driveway will have an impact on the expectations of an arriving dinner guest depending on whether he associates it with status and security, or ostentation and self-indulgence.

Our purposes for being in a setting often influence which elements are selected for attention. For instance, Erving Goffman describes how white-collar business people have an image of office buildings as being made up of floor spaces, offices, lobbies, and elevators, whereas:

> . . . janitors and scrubwomen have a clear perception of the small doors that lead to the back regions of business buildings and are intimately familiar with the profane transportation system for transporting dirty cleaning equipment, large stage props, and themselves.
>
> (Erving Goffman, *The Presentation of Self in Everyday Life*)

This patterning of perception is one reason why being at the office at an unusual time, such as on a Sunday morning, can jog a person to see some of the invisible elements that were never noticed before.

The classic difference in expectations and perceptions of settings may be that between residents and visitors. Residents see their settings as living histories of their experiences, struggles, and accomplishments, while visitors see the same setting through eyes that have very different sets of expectations and responsibilities (or, more usually, lack of responsibilities). An obvious example is the different sense of place between Caribbean resort hotel employees and the lounging tourists who are guests; or the place experiences of tired home owners versus weekend guests who admire large gardens that they don't have to tend.

Unconscious Orientations

Some of the expectations we bring to a setting are unconscious—we are aware neither of them, nor of the patterns that they create in our behavior. For example, we often develop unconscious but consistent orientations toward certain directions and away from others. When traveling, we may consistently use the areas near our hotel that were first explored (and therefore became comfortable to us), even though other directions may hold more potentially interesting features.

Orientations also shape the expectations of neighborhood residents. One study found that housewives in Cambridge, England tended to prefer to go to shops that were in the direction of the center of town rather than away from it, even though this would sometimes mean traveling a greater distance than if they went to shops in the opposite direction.[1] Residents of areas near major mountains or rivers orient themselves toward these features that play a dominant role in their lives through influencing weather and land use. Claude Levi-Strauss has suggested that cities develop westward (possibly as if following the sun); residents of modern cities are often oriented to move in certain unvarying paths and directions so that there may be interesting areas quite near to them that they have never seen.

Is this vacant lot a place of opportunity or a problem? It depends on whether you are a kid with a Frisbee or a maintenance person charged with keeping it litter-free.

PERSONAL PROCESSES: WHAT PEOPLE BRING TO THEIR SETTINGS

Exclusive Uses Another type of unconscious expectation is the tendancy to assume that a particular setting is only for specific purposes, thereby under-using its other possibilities. Nan Fairbrother provides a nice example:

> Indeed one of the most important forms of multiple use of land and resources in the future is surely the development of cities as recreation areas. Cities at present are chiefly where we work not play—except of course when we are abroad and cities immediately become holiday magnets. And this could equally happen at home: especially for people who live away from the centre. Here are the same shops and restaurants and gardens and parks and culture and entertainment—all the attractions in fact which we value abroad (and which visitors value here).

(Nan Fairbrother, *New Lives, New Landscapes*)

I have experienced exactly what she describes, and I know that my own assumptions block me from using my home city of Boston in the free ways in which I use foreign cities when I am traveling. The first step to richer use is to recognize in ourselves these consistent expectations that catch us in unvarying, habitual uses of the setting, and thereby reduce the richness of our sense of that place.

The effects of expectations are not all negative, of course. They allow us to structure our behavior efficiently in many regular situations, so that we do not have to rediscover the function of every element in every new setting. It is sometimes quite nice to know that a door with a sign on it saying Gentlemen or Ladies can solve an immediate physiological problem, so that one does not have to wander around trying various doors in the hope of success. Conversely, inappropriate expectations can also get you into trouble in a new setting. From their experiences at home, European visitors to American cities expect to be able to find public lavatories that are visible and accessible; they find out the hard way that this is not so, by doing some very bad (or ultimately painful) planning of their days on the streets.

Not a perfect expectation-setting name for drawing people to this spot to eat. . . .

There are still advantages to accurate expectations, however, especially in settings in which stress might be high. One environmental study found that scientists working in the Arctic adapted better to the harsh environment if they had a strong sense of purpose, including both why they were there and what the setting could provide to help them achieve their goals.[2] Thus expectations not only channel perceptions, they can provide structure for our experiences as a whole, and can be a force for survival in a demanding setting.

THE MAGIC OF MOODS

The other internal influence on our sense of place can be called broadly, mood: the immediate emotional state we bring to a setting, such as feeling generally good or troubled, excited or placid, secure or anxious, tense or relaxed, happy or sad, and so forth. Thus mood acts as a filter on how we see, feel about, and react to elements in our physical and social surroundings. This is no doubt a familiar idea to most. What may be less obvious is the amount of influence our moods have on our *view* of the setting, so that what we think is an unbiased picture of the world is really a product of time, place, and frame of mind.

My favorite description of the influence of mood comes from an early P. G. Wodehouse novel, where Lord Emsworth's secretary, the Efficient Baxter, finds himself inadvertently locked out of Blandings Castle in the middle of the night:

> In the Middle Ages . . . Blandings had been an impregnable fortress, but in all its career it can seldom have looked more of a fortress than it did now to the Efficient Baxter.
>
> One of the disadvantages of being a man of action, impervious to the softer emotions, is that in moments of trial the beauties of Nature are powerless to soothe the anguished heart. Had Baxter been of a dreamy and poetic temperament he might now have been drawing all sorts of balm from the loveliness of his surroundings. The air was full of the scent of growing things; strange, shy creatures came and went about him as he walked; down in the woods a nightingale had begun to sing; and there was something grandly majestic in the huge bulk of the castle as it towered against the sky. But Baxter had temporarily lost his sense of smell; he feared and disliked the strange shy creatures; the nightingale left him cold; and the only thought the towering castle inspired in him was that it looked as if a fellow would need half a ton of dynamite to get into it.
>
> (P. G. Wodehouse, *Leave it to Psmith*)

Not only beauty is in the eyes of the beholder, so is just about every other evaluative dimension when it comes to how one feels about a setting. Blandings Castle on the afternoon before Baxter's nocturnal wanderings probably felt to him like a sleepy setting in which a person could get a bit of work done and still not lose touch with longer-term traditional values in life.

A more common case today is the ubiquitous urban traffic jam. What kind of "place" this is depends on whether the driver is nervous about being late for an appointment, or relaxed and thereby able to enjoy the opportunity to look at things along the route that are usually not seen because they are passed at 30 or 40 miles per hour. Similarly, many tourists never notice that the variations in the quality of their place experiences depend on how tired, interested, or happy they are when they visit different places on their itinerary. They generally describe their experiences as having been "caused" by the spot itself being good or bad, interesting or drab, and seldom realize that their mood was such that any setting would have seemed dull or beautiful. In many instances, travelers should visit a spot three or four times, when they are in different moods, if they wish to be able really to describe what that setting can offer.

During a period when I was temporarily living in London and feeling discouraged by my lack of progress in writing, I felt that I had totally explored the city, and that there was nothing interesting left to discover there. As I began to feel better about my work, I also discovered unknown fascinating areas of the city. When pressed, I will admit that London did not really change all that much in the space of a week or two, but my perceptions of it certainly did, being reshaped by how I was feeling about myself and my work. It was also a circular process, as my apathetic mood led me not to go out and explore (it was too much trouble), thereby ensuring that I would not discover new interests in the city, thus confirming my view that there was nothing left to discover, and so on. We create part of our own place reality by the behavioral choices we make when we are in certain moods.

Settings sometimes violate our expectations; we could expect a quick mood change when this car's driver returns to it.

Because the influence process is circular, a strongly positive setting can also help to overcome a bad mood and thus improve our sense of place. Each reader probably has a favorite setting that can lift his or her spirits, just by being in it for a while. The point is a simple one: our experiences in a setting are factors that shape our moods, just as our moods help to shape our experiences in settings. On Colin Fletcher's first day of his epic hike through the Grand Canyon, he had to make a risky and uncertain swim across the Colorado River; this experience in an unknown setting had an immediate effect on his mood:

> The cold no longer mattered, though, I knew it would pass. But when I looked back up into the silent and somber Gorge, I saw that although the gloom had by now grown deeper, the evening was no longer gloomy; and I knew that merely because I had crossed the back eddy and then had returned, the Gorge would never again seem quite such a terrible place. And I knew that this new response would last.

> (Colin Fletcher, *The Man Who Walked Through Time*)

In this case, Fletcher's gloomy sense of place was clearly due in part to uncertainty about how he would be able to handle physical challenges in a difficult environment. Trying to do something difficult early in the trip and succeeding, had a real payoff by reducing this uncertainty and freeing him to focus on opportunities instead of just on problems. Thus by doing something that affected his mood, he improved his accumulating place experiences throughout the trip. His appreciation of the setting would have been much less if he had worried throughout the trip, and then done something that improved his mood so that he could enjoy the setting just as he was going out of the Canyon.

A different type of mood influence occurs when we have a particularly strong experience or feelings in a setting, and then return to that setting at a later time. A sight, an odor, or a sound can set off the feelings we had there before, and may flip us right back into the mood of that time. We will say more about this effect in Chapter 14 (on memories), as it is really caused by qualities of the setting, but I mention it here because it is also caused by the associations with previous events that we bring with us.

To conclude, I would like to share two simple strategies for how to enrich place experiences while traveling in a new area.

Choosing a Focus Travel experiences can be sharpened and enriched considerably by our intentions. Obviously, one focus is to just go to see the sights, but this often results in a relatively predictable round of visits to spots that we have read about a dozen times; when we are through, our trip does not have any real personality to distinguish it from one anyone might have taken.

An alternative is literally to "choose a focus," that is, to select some tasks, questions, or types of items to seek out while on the trip. This structure will then lead to a chain of steps, somewhat like that constructed by an investigative reporter on the trail of a story, and will result in one's having seen areas

A visitor's mood would determine whether she would see this dog comfort station in Boston's Waterfront Park as useful, a frivolous waste of tax money, or funny.

and people that would never have been noticed on the standard tour. For example, if you have an interest in art, instead of just going to the obvious galleries and museums when visiting London, you might choose to look for Whistler etchings in smaller print shops. You could get some advice from a gallery on where to start; these would suggest others in less well-known parts of the city, who would suggest still others; and so on. You would end up with a range of interesting experiences with maps, means of transportation, and different neighborhoods, including some only known to residents. You might or might not end up owning some new Whistler etchings, but the real measure of success would be your experiences, not your purchases.

The actual content of the focusing task does not really make much difference, as long as you have some enthusiasm for it. What matters is the structure that starts you in unpredictable directions, so that your place experiences are not so biased by your expectations. I have heard of people searching the New York sewing machine district for spare parts and discovering new worlds there; I have friends who dig into the history and present social structure of the small towns they visit in rural America; and so on. As long as the beginning focus is of some interest, and is related to the setting so that there is a place to start looking, it can greatly enrich your travel experiences.

Psychological Investment   The second suggestion is aimed at influencing your mood when you are traveling. It is to make a basic psychological investment in your trip: to commit yourself to putting in at least minimum resources that will be required to use the settings well and make the trip worthwhile. This process requires you to think consciously about what will be required of you in time, energy, money, attention, courage, or whatever, to have an exciting, fulfilling trip. If this is done, your expectations and mood will both be more likely to allow you to enjoy the places you visit.

Foreign travel today provides a classic example. You can react to a (seemingly) never-ending series of expenditures—transportation, porters' tips, taxis, hotels, meals, souvenirs—as a long series of illegitimate demands being made on you, or as one predictable demand that was incurred when you decided to take the trip. People who react to each demand as a new affront have not made this psychological investment; as a result, they fret over costs, make themselves miserable, and blame this mood on the place rather than on their own orientation to the trip. Our place experiences are somewhat less than enriching if our main memory of a taxi ride through the center of Paris is watching the meter click over and trying continuously to convert it from francs to dollars. If that's the mood, we are paying twice for the ride: in the money we spent, and in the new things that went unnoticed because we were so concerned about the money. Our memories of the place will really be mainly memories of the rather foul mood we were in as we passed through; for that we could have stayed home and saved on both costs.

NOTES

1. T. R. Lee, "Perceived Distance as a Function of Direction in the City," *Environment and Behavior*, Vol. 2, No. 1, 1970, pp. 40–51.
2. F. Pope and T. Rogers, "Some Psychiatric Aspects of Arctic Survival Experiments," *Journal of Nervous and Mental Disease*, Vol. 146, 1968, pp. 433–455.

5 Personal Preferences and Place People

A third major factor that people bring to settings is personal preferences: those enduring interests and enthusiasms that guide a person's focuses and choices in relating to the world. It is obvious that people differ in what they find to be interesting and gratifying. This is one reason why everyone in the United States does not end up on the same California beach on the same summer day (although it may seem that way to those who do).

For our purpose here, I will risk oversimplifying and suggest that styles of personal preference tend to fall into three broad types, roughly corresponding to the old trio of things, people, and places. That is, "things people" are particularly interested in the things they do, their work and other activities; *what* they are doing is the most important determinant of whether they are feeling all right. They may be very concerned about things that they amass, and therefore seem to be creating a particular environment; but their interest stems from things as indicators of the success of their activities. "People people," on the other hand, seem to be most influenced by *whom* they are doing things with; their relationships are of primary importance, and their activities can be almost anything as long as their satisfactory relationships are not restricted. These two types obviously lead into the third type, "place people," who find their most consistent satisfactions from the ways in which they relate to their immediate surroundings, through exploring, traveling, reshaping their settings, and so on. For them, the *where* of their action is generally more interesting than what it is or with whom it happens.

These differences become clear when there is a mismatch, such as a dating relationship between a people person and a place person. The former wants to share experiences and work on the relationship, while the latter often reluctantly agrees to this, *provided* it can be done in the appropriate setting, such as a nice walk through leafy suburban streets on a spring evening. The people person will feel miffed at the concern about such a "trivial" matter as where they talk, while the place person will feel that the encounter is mushy and sticky and will be wasted time unless spent in a good location.

This book is not really the medium for exploring this highly simplified notion about personal preferences. I will however, explore and expand on the concept of a place person in the rest of this chapter.

WHAT ARE PLACE PEOPLE?

In a very interesting book called *Topophilia*[1] (literally, "love of place"), Yi-Fu Tuan described the strong force created by a person's emotional attachment to a particular area (what he called a place, but I would call a setting). Although I think that place people are probably more likely to feel such attachments, this love of a place is not a necessary part of the basic definition of a place person. It does not hinge on liking a particular setting, but on liking the process of interaction between one's self and one's setting, on being fascinated by or drawn to the sense of place experience.

This *looks* like the house of a place person, but we would have to know more about how it got that way. It may just be cared for by a place person.

PERSONAL PROCESSES: WHAT PEOPLE BRING TO THEIR SETTINGS

Place people, therefore, do not just love their settings, they have a variety of ways of showing their interest in them. They may receive great satisfaction out of discovering new settings, exploring, and finding out what goes on in them. They have strongly biased feelings for or against certain locations without articulating why. They are sensitive to their own situation in and orientation to a setting, being aware of things, people, and events there that are not directly related to their own activity. Even when they hate a setting, they may still be interested in the fact that they feel so strongly about it, while non–place people would just want to leave.

Some place people are able to perceive cues and atmosphere that are not visible to most others. For example, members of certain American Indian tribes are able to "feel" the location of ancient grave sites on the open plains, even though there are no grave markers as such.[2] Place people also tend to care more about having stimulating place experiences, to get more out of them, and to resent settings that are sterile or bland. They may go into occupations (see Chapter 11) that allow rich place experiences through job organization or travel opportunities.

Although place people may be better at dealing with their settings, the essence of my definition is not their competence, but their interest in the place experience. They find it inherently interesting and valuable. This interest can be manifested fairly indirectly, such as a consultant who seems to travel in order to serve a scattered group of clients, but actually chooses to work in far-flung locations in order to travel and explore new settings. By contrast, non–place people will focus on what they are doing or with whom they are doing it, and be aware of the setting only when it is not working well.

This last point suggests that strong feelings about settings come from somewhat opposite sources for place and non–place people. For the former, sense of place satisfies. By contrast, those in the other two categories become aware mainly as the settings dissatisfy, that is, the place experience usually becomes important to them only when it drops below some minimal standard that does not support their activities and/or relationships, which provide their real satisfaction. These are not hard and fast rules, of course, but patterns that tend to distingish the three types of life interests.

WHAT DO PLACE PEOPLE LIKE?

Place people can often be spotted by their obsessions—those blessed afflictions that often drive them to behave in ways that make little sense to the other types. These obsessions can take a variety of forms, some important, some trivial, some consistent, and others contradictory:

- Exploring unknown settings
- Using or just looking at maps
- Fixing or tinkering with their settings
- Wandering wherever impulse takes them
- Observing and discussing designs, both architectural and interior

Boston Common from the air: such views are inherently interesting to place people.

- Hiking, walking, and running (in both city and country)
- Changing homes fairly frequently
- Keeping home locations for a long time
- Seeing settings while traveling—gawking out of airplane, car, or train windows
- Reading books that have a strong spirit of place

The list of interests could be long, and of course, no one gets a special joy out of all of them. People develop different patterns of interests and ways of expressing them. Some place people write about their experiences, such as John Hillaby's books about walking explorations,[3] or write fiction about their particular locale. Others develop special adaptive skills: P. G. Wodehouse was able to work in and be stimulated by almost any setting, including a wartime internment camp in France (he carried his place with him, in his head), while his wife Ethel became skilled in quickly creating a new home when they moved, which was frequently in their middle years.[4] Thoreau described a place person as knowing his roads and fields; while in a book called *The Poetics of Space*, Gaston Bachelard wrote about the place person as "a dreamer of houses" being enchanted by experiences with both real and imagined homes.

Sometimes place people become obsessed with particular spots, so that they will do almost anything to experience being in them, while non–place people would write off this feeling as reflecting an interesting possibility that probably could not be realized. For Edward Abbey, the vehicular descent into a dangerous remote canyon area in Utah called The Maze, had the quality of a religious pilgrimage:

PERSONAL PROCESSES: WHAT PEOPLE BRING TO THEIR SETTINGS

Now, after the recent rains, which were also responsible for the amazing growth of grass and flowers we have seen, we find the trail marvelously eroded, stripped of all vestiges of soil, trenched and gullied down to bare rock, in places more like a stairway than a road. Even if we can get the Land Rover down this thing, how can we ever get it back up again?

But it doesn't occur to either of us to back away from the attempt. We are determined to get into the Maze. Waterman has great confidence in his machine; and further more, as with anything enormously attractive, we are obsessed only with getting *in*; we can worry later about getting out.

(Edward Abbey, *Desert Solitaire*)

Only a true place person could see the terrible road, the main obstacle to their safe return, as "marvelously eroded," and the whole unknown depths as "enormously attractive."

Another passion is maps. They bring out the real obsessiveness of place people, and provide a sense of joy and intrigue that seems completely disproportionate to others. The reasons for this fascination are fairly clear. Maps are representations of settings and the relationships among their features. As such, they allow one to engage in armchair travel experiences: to fantasize; to solve puzzles that increase understanding of how a setting is organized; and to solidify understanding of an area by reviewing it on a map after exploring it. All of these sound like fairly dry and logical attractions for map-lovers, but the real point is that maps are fun for such a person, and I mean almost any map showing almost any setting, from the scale of the earth as a whole down to a map of one's own backyard.

Another pleasure for the place person is random exploring; not aiming at a particular, known-by-reputation spot such as the Maze, but just wandering and finding out what is to be discovered. When place people are house guests, their love for getting the feel of a new setting can bring them into conflict with their hosts, who feel called on to show them around the commonly defined noteworthy features of their setting, such as historic buildings, fanciest neighborhoods, or famous battle sites. Ironically, the visitors want to see whatever is there, not just the sights. They want to experience the setting, not their hosts' image of what it ought to be. Vacant lots or gas stations can provide more of the real feel of a town than its main civic buildings.

There is an interesting pattern suggested by these examples. A number of them have to do with having choices or options and the opportunity to use them when appropriate. Although I do not think that being a place person is limited to those who are financially well-off, this pattern suggests that being a satisfied place person may be more characteristic of those in upper economic brackets, who are more likely to have grown up with options, to have the resources to change locations, and to tinker with their settings and control significant aspects of them. Even this general trend would have exceptions, however. Hobos are freer to change settings and explore new territory than are most of those who must or who choose to work for a living, but it is a mixed blessing. They are more free because they are bound by fewer social norms about where they should be and what responsibilities they should fulfill; but lack of resources can be a considerable constraint on mobility.

PLACE PEOPLE AND COMPETENCE

Are place people, because of their inherent interest in the process of experiencing places, more likely to be competent in dealing with their settings? I do not have a definitive answer, but my suspicion is that on the average they would have more place-related skills because they seek more opportunities to develop and practice them.

These skills could take several different forms, however. One is a sensitivity to the qualities (magical and practical) of settings, which allows one to make good choices about locations and how to use them. For example, Louis and Mary Leakey spent over thirty years, many of them "unproductive," searching for traces of humanity's prehistoric ancestors in the Olduvai Gorge in East Africa. Their commitment and patience led eventually to some spectacular discoveries. These successes may be partly because of some physical indications that the location was right, but it seemed that much of their determination to search there rested on intuition, a sensitivity to the spirit of place that focused them on the Gorge rather than somewhere else, despite frequent criticism from their colleagues implying that their choice was crazy.

A second likely skill of place people can be called "custodianship": the rich but nondestructive use of one's settings. There seem to be whole *place cultures* that produce people who value place experiences, and who are more skilled at nondestructively relating to their settings. The Hopi Indians of the American Southwest are an example:

> Such a tradition, like many other versions of its kind, marked the relationship of the Hopis to the land. . . . The land was not tangible property to be owned, divided, and alienated at will. It was their Mother Earth from which they were born, on whose breast they were suckled, and to whose womb they were returned in a prenatal posture at death. . . . Hence the Indians did not see themselves apart from all other physical forms of life. They regarded themselves as a part of one living whole.
>
> (Frank Waters, *Pumpkin Seed Point*)

Further on, Waters contrasts this place-culture ability to relate to nature with the western European things culture tradition:

> The Christian-European white race, from its first discovery of this pristine New World of the red race, regarded it as one vast new treasure house of inanimate nature that existed solely to be exploited for the material welfare of man.

We would expect this latter tradition to produce fewer place persons who are skillfully able to relate to their settings, as contrasted with attempting to dominate the settings over the long run. In the United States, this stance of domination is horribly visible in the often condemned (but seldom altered) practice of bulldozing a site's features into a flat pan as a way of "preparing" for simplified building. Whatever features the site possessed have been consid-

Cats are often described as place animals; they seem generally to pick their spots well for what they are doing.

ered irrelevant compared with the wonderful spirit the new building is supposed to provide; occasionally, the developers wonder why the place somehow does not feel as interesting as their plans projected that it would.

What are the implications of personal preference patterns that lead people to be consistently more or less aware of their own sense of place? Let me summarize a few of the main points: place people bring different (and often more varied) expectations to a setting than non–place people; place people value the sense of place experience for its own sake, not just as a means to some other end related to tasks or relationships; they make life choices based on place considerations, caring about not only *where* they should be, but also about the *process* for making decisions on location, and they find these decisions to be opportunities rather than unavoidable hassles (which is how non–place people feel about them); as we will discuss in more detail later, place people are drawn to occupations that allow them some scope for exploration, tinkering, wandering, and the like, so that they combine earning a living with pleasurable place experiences.

Having made these distinctions, I would like to finish by backing off slightly. The tone of this chapter has probably led readers to conclude that I believe that being a place person is something one tends to be born with. In fact, I am not at all sure that this is the case. Although I am sure that some people are born with the tendency, I am also sure that almost every human being

A delicatessen to warm the hearts of place people in San Francisco.

is born with some natural curiosity about the world. It is the combination of opportunities, encouragements, and experiences that people have as they grow up that determines the value they put on sense of place. If we are aware of this, and if we believe (as I do) that the development of a sensitivity to place experiences is a good thing, we can help to foster this in our children and the other people on whom we have an impact.

This view also suggests all of us are at least latent place people, and that using our settings better and getting more joy out of them are learnable, practicable skills that can, in fact, be developed if we try. The last few chapters of this book are designed to provide some ways to do this and are based on the fundamental assumption that guides this whole book: understanding the sense of place and how it occurs can lead to better experiences and a more significant impact on our world.

In the end, the moral sentiment for self-improvement is not what this chapter is all about. It is simply about the special fun that a place person has when striking that spark in relation to a setting:

> I used to like movie theatres, especially up to about the age of twenty-eight. And I used to like the theatre, where plays were performed on the stage, but that also has become something neither enjoyed nor needed.
>
> Best of all, best of all is a long street in a city, and myself upon it walking at my leisure to see what's there.
>
> (William Saroyan, *Places Where I've Done Time*)

NOTES

1. Yi-Fu Tuan, *Topohilia*, Englewood Cliffs, N.J.: Prentice-Hall, 1974.

2. T. C. McLuhan, *Touch the Earth, A Self-Portrait of Indian Existence*, New York: Promontory Press, 1971, p. 7.

3. For example, John Hillaby, *Journey through Europe*, St. Albans, Herts, UK: Paladin, 1974.

4. David Jasen, *P. G. Wodehouse: A Portrait of a Master*, New York: Mason and Lipscomb, 1974, pp. 197, 205.

PART THREE

WHAT SETTING BRINGS TO PLACE

6

The Spirit of Place: Finding the Blue Haze

Although people's own characteristics make a major contribution to their sense of place, settings provide the other input. Some settings have features that give them a special spirit of place, or personality that draws similar reactions from different users. This section of the book explores several aspects of this spirit, including physical features, social climate, elements of mystery, city diseases, and personal traces left by a particular user or owner. The main theme is that there are settings with such strong, distinct qualities that they are more likely than bland settings to stimulate a noticable sense of place. In considering the role of physical aspects I have selected several potent features as examples: strong location, boundaries, geographic distinctiveness, scale and proportion, and rich identity and imagery.

STRONG LOCATION

Strong location refers to a setting's placement in geographic space: where it is and how it relates to its surroundings. For instance, a small Colorado town that can only be reached by two days of travel on tortuous mountain backroads would have a different feel than a visually identical town reached by a three-hour drive from Denver. The experiences in reaching them are obviously different. In addition, previous experiences of persons arriving in the remote town are likely to be more similar than are the experiences of those arriving by various routes to the accessible town.

To choose one of my favorite examples, there are many spots in England's Yorkshire dales that seem to have this quality of special location that affects how people arrive there. As one author described it:

> The most impressive approach to a view of one of the dales is to come upon it from the high moors—what the dalesfolk call, so expressively, from off the 'tops'. One has spent the day, perhaps, up in this world of heather, with grouse or curlew providing a commentary to one's every movement, and with wide views of moorland cut by faint runnels and gullies, many of which are, in fact, the gaps of the dale lip seen in foreshortened perspective. The high ground begins to decline and one may come to the edge of the heather and peat and enter a world of benty grass and occasional stream heads. Then comes the moment when one looks 'over the edge'—the convexity of the hill has reached the point where one can look back up the gentler slope of moorland, or forward down what often appears to be an almost precipitious slope into the valley.

> (Arthur Raistrick, *The Pennine Dales*)

I am not sure how much this passage communicates to one who has not already had that experience, but to one who has, it immediately recalls a number of potent place experiences while walking over moorland that one might carelessly assume had no particularly special areas. The distinctions are created by relative locations of features, such as soft hills, rocky ledges, and undulating bogs, and the resulting sequence in which they are experienced while one goes walking among them.

Locational impact is particularly potent when the key feature of the setting is in strong contrast to its immediate surroundings. The experience of two different sets of stimuli in close relationship heightens our awareness of ourselves in a place. A desert with mountains visible nearby is a different place than one without them; and hills that rise directly out of the sea can look much more majestic than higher peaks that are part of a generally mountainous area; for example, San Francisco's hills are more prominent because of their relationship to the bay.

Consider the spirit of place through contrast in a small Eskimo village:

> In a way the Ihalmiut camp seemed only to accentuate the apparent desolation and emptiness of the artic plains, and yet in the immediate vicinity of the tents was this little pocket of life in the center of the human vacuum that otherwise possessed the Barrens.

> (Farley Mowat, *People of the Deer*)

WHAT SETTING BRINGS TO PLACE

Certain American cities' spirits are shaped by their geography and how people have adapted to it (San Francisco).

The same village on the edge of metropolitan Toronto would, of course, not be the same village. The contrast with the Barrens makes it feel much richer and more human, while being near Toronto would make it feel primitive and somewhat shabby by comparison with newer sections.

Cities such as London, that have small parks and green squares scattered about, provide a good instance of the spirit created by contrast. A small square may be beautiful in its own right, but it is all the more delightful when one has just turned a corner and left the noise and bustle of city traffic.

BOUNDARIES

Another familiar physical factor in creating a spirit of place is *boundaries,* a clear delineation of a setting from its surroundings. They may be on a small scale, such as arrangements of furniture in the home that create a distinct area from the rest of a room. They may be on an intermediate scale, such as walls, fences, or hedges around a group of buildings, creating a clear identity as a compound or enclave. Boundaries at this level create " . . . the alleys, cul-de-sacs, quiet courts, colorful marketplaces, nostalgic neighborhoods, secluded streets," that are loved as special places in a large city.[1]

On a still larger scale, some entire towns and cities have a spirit of place and are not just collections of settings; this spirit is often enhanced by clear boundaries. Paris appears to be an example, as its residents have an image of the boundaries as formed by both the ancient town walls and the modern ring expressway.[2] Areas within a large city may also have boundaries, such as major roads, rivers, or other barriers to pedestrian movement, and are therefore more likely to be perceived as distinct places. The Greenwich Village section of New York City is such a setting, as is the North End (Italian-American) in Boston. The boundaries around the North End are primarily heavily traveled roadways, as they are for the Covent Garden area of London.

THE SPIRIT OF PLACE: FINDING THE BLUE HAZE

The architectural term that is frequently used in conjunction with boundaries is "enclosure": the closing-in effect of physical features, which in the right circumstances helps to create a special spirit of place. London's Victorian covered shopping malls such as Burlington Arcade or Piccadilly Arcade have this quality. So does the Leadenhall Market area, where a street intersection was covered to create a special easily identifiable (but sometimes hard to find in the maze of streets) location.

As Oscar Newman demonstrated in his analysis of physical features that lead one to identify a setting as one's own and defend it from intruders, the boundary does not have to be physically secure (e.g., a high wall or 30-yard zone of rolled barbed wire); the most important requirement for generating a sense of identification is that the boundary be symbolically clear, so that there is an obvious difference between inside and outside:

> Some represent real barriers: U-shaped buildings, high walls and fences, and locked gates and doors. Others are symbolic barriers only: open gateways, light standards, a short run of steps, planting, and changes in the texture of the walking surface. Both serve a common purpose: to inform that one is passing from a space which is public where one's presence is not questioned through a barrier to a space which is private and where one's presence requires justification.
>
> (Oscar Newman, *Defensible Space*)

(Courtesy of the British Tourist Authority)

Enclosure, human scale, and visual variety: London's Burlington Arcade.

WHAT SETTING BRINGS TO PLACE

Spirit of place is very clearly created by entrance gate and visible name, so that there is no doubt about the boundary between inside and and outside.

Note that the boundary's communication serves a purpose in messages both to the stranger, who knows when he is moving into private space, and to the resident, who must know where the territory is and feel identified with it in order to know when to take defensive action.

Similarly, the major contributor to effective territorial defense in animals has been shown to be establishment of symbolic boundaries that allow the animal at home to feel confident while inside them, and to identify when intrusion has occurred. The actual boundary markers may be natural features (streams, trees, bushes, rocks) or alterations by the home animal (a dug track, a trail of urine, and so on). It does not make too much difference, so long as resident and visitor both recognize the cues.

GEOGRAPHIC DISTINCTIVENESS

One of the most visible traits that create a special aura for a setting is, of course, geographic distinctiveness. Examples of this effect are so well known that I will just make a few brief points here.

Countries sometimes become known for a spirit of place through their geographic features. Not all have this spirit, and in fact a good many countries are little more than political divisions. The countries that do have such a spirit

(Courtesy of the Scottish Tourist Board)

Striking features: a loch in Scotland.

usually have special distinguishing features. Scotland's hills and lochs are obvious examples, along with Algeria's desert, and France's fertile wine-producing regions. Popular historian Alan Moorehead once wrote that every special country has at least one distinguishing feature that is so typical that visitors always sense it and residents do not even remark on it. For him, Kenya's feature was the blue haze, which

> . . . haunts the early morning and the evening, and it gives one an intense feeling of liberation, of immense uncharted distances through which one would like to go on moving indefinitely, and without object, simply letting the time go by.
>
> (Alan Moorehead, *No Room in the Ark*)

Special settings also attract people who are particularly attuned to their dominant features, such as beach lovers to California, so that the setting is made up of both interesting features and people who are excited by and drawn to them, thus creating a doubly strong identity for the setting. Travel writer Jan Morris wrote an interesting piece exploring the drawing power of settings that have water in almost any form—seashore, rivers, lakes, ponds, canals, and so on.[3] Those who love water will always find it somewhere, thus creating a special social as well as physical climate. The cry, "Surf's up!" does not mean much to the average resident of Topeka, but it is music to the ears of the Santa Monica set.

WHAT SETTING BRINGS TO PLACE

For a country as large as the United States, there cannot really be one distinctive geographic spirit of place, so particular regions develop a strong identity if their features stand out enough. A few obvious examples are the Badlands of South Dakota, Canyon lands in Utah, the Everglades in Florida, and Cape Cod in Massachusetts. The fact that I can refer to each of these areas with names that bring immediate images to mind, merely underscores the distinctiveness of their spirit. Sometimes the special feature is not a single element, but a relationship among several, such as earth and sky in the Great Plains of Kansas and Nebraska.

Distinctiveness also cuts across national boundaries, so that there is sometimes a certain spirit of place that is similar in a number of countries. One example is the spine of North American mountains that runs up through Mexico, the United States, and Canada. It is a powerful region that binds together its residents, and leads them to share a sense of place with one another more than they do with fellow countrymen who live in different regions. A resident of the Canadian Rockies would have a view of the world more like that of a Mexican mountain dweller than that of a resident of New Brunswick or Nova Scotia.

SCALE AND PROPORTION

Another potent feature concerns the scale of environmental elements. Certain size relationships combine to create a special effect. For instance, travel writer James Morris has pointed out that the small Indian hill station of Darjeeling impresses visitors as being almost magically tiny because of the setting in which it is seen: the towering massiveness of the Himalyan Mountain range, whose proportions are not like any other geographical feature on the face of the earth. This effect of large elements making the small to appear still smaller suggests to me that the impact of scale can be made by bigness, by smallness, or by some surprising mix between the two. Places whose spirit is defined by their bigness include cities such as Paris, Rome, New York, London, Tokyo, and so on; mountain areas such as the Alps and the Himalayas; and America's Grand Canyon.

Some large buildings, such as New York's Empire State Building, the Pentagon, the Astrodome, or St. Peter's in Rome, take on an identity that is strongly based on their scale in relation to the people using them; in fact, the intention of the builders was often to communicate the infinite smallness of humans through such settings. The advent of new building technologies has created many more huge buildings, so that their impact is now less unusual. I would guess, however, that the cumulative impact of very large buildings is to reinforce people's sense of smallness and powerlessness without offering much hope (as did the great cathedrals) as to what they can identify with in order to reduce their insignificance.

Smallness and spirit of place: Acorn St. on Boston's Beacon Hill.

Smallness as a contributor to personality is exemplified by intimate rooms in homes; entertainment places such as small cafes (where the smallness is partly achieved by a low light level that makes it difficult to see much beyond one's companion); cave dwellings, such as those in the Southwest region of the United States; and children's play houses and other private hideaways.

RICH IMAGES

My last dimension is really a mixed physical and social one: the extent to which the setting is rich in features that conjure up images in users' minds. The connection between a feature and the images it creates is a learned one, based on both personal experiences and on cultural themes that are received over time. For example, Paris has been already mentioned as a city with a strong image because it has so many international symbols, that is, features (such as the *Arc de Triomphe* or the Eiffel Tower) that are recognizable by people throughout the world. Other cities include Venice, San Francisco, Amsterdam, New York, and London, each of which has characteristics that generate consistent images and therefore a strong spirit of place.

WHAT SETTING BRINGS TO PLACE

Strong images do not require large or cosmopolitan settings, of course. Medieval European towns with complex street patterns and traces of many generations of users generate a rich fabric of images and quite strong spirit of place. Some recent residential developments in the United States, such as Columbia, Maryland, have managed to incorporate imagery of pleasant, low-key town life through green areas, pedestrian and bike paths, and village centers, which in turn expresses a real sense of identity rather than simply placeless suburban sprawl.

In a study of city perceptions, *The Image of the City*, Kevin Lynch found several types of features that created a strong image (or a weak image when they were absent): *paths* along which people customarily move, with regular paths creating a clearer image; *edges,* which can be barriers, roads, water (see earlier discussion of boundaries); *districts,* which are the identifiable sections of a city, also discussed above; *nodes,* the strategic points in a city at which paths join, such as Fifth Avenue and 42nd Street in New York, or where activities are concentrated, such as the Loop in Chicago; and *landmarks*, physical objects that are both recognizable and visible enough from different vantage points to be used for orientation.[4]

In other words, a city rich in these features will have a strong spirit of place, and be remembered as such, and a city that lacks them will have a weak or confused image. An example of the latter is the borough of Queens in New York City:

> A resident of Queens is four times as likely to identify a street location in Manhattan than in his own borough (3.76% for his home borough of Queens versus 15% for Manhattan). Areas of Queens have often been accused of being non-descript, and taxi drivers are reputed to fear entering Queens lest they never find their way out.
>
> (Milgram, et al., "A Psychological Map of New York City," *American Scientist*, Vol. 60, No. 2, 1972, p. 199.)

Creating a spirit of place by design: sculpture as a landmark defining a spot as "somewhere."

THE SPIRIT OF PLACE: FINDING THE BLUE HAZE

It is that sense of being nowhere or anywhere that distinguishes the low-imagery setting from a rich-imagery one that is felt to be a definite somewhere.

In a later book, *What Time Is this Place?*, Lynch proposed several qualities of settings that contribute to good images of place: they are vivid and engaging; have a firm, resilient, and wide-ranging structure; and allow further exploration and development. His sense of "good" outcomes here is similar to our propositions in the first section of this book; that is, good rich images generate appropriate expectations about use, fantasies that enhance the place experience, and stimulation of perceptions of new alternatives for work and/or pleasure in the setting. These images also add to our internal storehouse of memories, so that in the future, our reveries are enhanced in the same or similar settings.

Having emphasized the main features that create a strong spirit of place, we should also be aware that many of the settings in which we spend time do not have any strong spirit. As we will discuss in later chapters, American settings in particular, seem to be headed toward greater and greater homogenization, with regional differences being wiped out by standardized architecture, malls, fast-food chains, and the like. In these characterless settings, sense of place would be primarily created by personal history, expectations, and mood, rather than by the strong spirit of the setting in combination with personal characteristics.

Our final point is a caution: saying that a setting has a strong spirit of place is not meant to imply that one always likes or has a preference for that setting. It is possible to perceive a setting as having a strong identity and to be neutral to it or dislike it. For example, people who have visited the Nazi death camp at Auschwitz in the last thirty years describe it as having an overwhelming spirit of place, an almost tangible aura of the souls who were murdered there, yet no one that I know of has reported liking the setting at all. Its spirit of place is strong, but also consistently negative and malevolent.

NOTES

1. For a nice collection of examples, see William H. Hemp, *New York Enclaves* (New York: Clarkson N. Potter, 1975).
2. Stanley Milgram and Denise Jodelet, "Psychological Maps of Paris," in H. Proshansky, W. Ittelson, and L. Rivlin, *Environmental Psychology: People and Their Physical Settings* (revised ed.), New York: Holt, Rinehart and Winston, 1976, p. 107.
3. Jan Morris, "On Wateriness," in *Travels*, London and New York: Harcourt Brace Jovanovich, 1976.
4. Kevin Lynch, *The Image of the City*, Cambridge, Mass.: The MIT Press, 1960 (especially Chapter 3).

7

The Sociography
of Place:
Doers and Watchers

If the physical features of a setting can be loosely called its geography, the social factors that contribute to its spirit of place can be called its sociography: the impact of other people's presence and their activities in and expectations for that setting. This chapter will consider several types of social influence: of individuals, collections, types, and social climate.

THE IMPACT OF INDIVIDUALS

The simplest contribution to a setting's spirit is a single individual's character. For example, novelist Anthony Powell describes the mark Nick Jenkins' Uncle Giles tended to make on any hotel he inhabited:

> Later when the Bellevue hove into sight—the nautical phrase is deliberately chosen—I saw at once that, during his visits there, Uncle Giles had irrevocably imposed his own personality upon the hotel. Standing at the corner of a short bleak, anonymous street some little way from the sea-front, this corner house, although much smaller in size, was otherwise scarcely to be distinguished from the Ufford, his London *pied-a-terre*. . . . Perhaps I attributed too much to his

powers of will. The physical surroundings of most individuals, left to their own choice, vary little wherever they happen to live.

(Anthony Powell, *The Kindly Ones*)

I agree with Powell's notion that a setting that carries the stamp of a person's character usually has this flavor for both reasons: the chosen setting more or less fits, and the person can influence its atmosphere to make it fit even more. (We discuss this in detail in the chapter on "Personal Places.")

I am sure that we have all had experiences with a setting whose spirit was shaped by an individual; many readers have probably been responsible for setting such a tone themselves. A less typical experience is the spirit of place created by a person in high power or with so-called star quality. Dick Cavett recalled this process as he observed it while working on Jack Paar's staff of the Tonight Show:

> It was a little like living at home with an alcoholic parent. The family's (staff's) first question was always 'How does he seem today?' I for one, when I finally came to terms with it, found it enormously interesting and stimulating, and watching the other staff members gird for it was an amusement in itself. As you once pointed out, the relationship of a star and his staff is essentially that of a king and his courtiers.

(Dick Cavett and Christopher Porterfield, *Cavett*)

Wherever the star is located, there is a special climate, partly because of the force of personality and partly because of the force of others' dependence. If one's livelihood depends on the good graces of one particular (and temperamental) person, that person's moods and actions become the most important features of setting, and small changes in either will be noticed and magnified immediately. Sense of place is narrowly focused on that person's influence, and most physical details in the setting fade into the background.

The feel of a setting is partly communicated by (subtle or not so subtle) clues about how past users and administrators have treated it.

WHAT SETTING BRINGS TO PLACE

A second influence is an individual's actual alteration of the setting that changes or sharpens its spirit of place. Such tinkering is often an attempt to control others' behavior there, such as when a farmer puts up a "no trespassing" sign on a footpath through his property and influences the mood of walkers who pass that point. Even if the walkers continue on, they feel differently about the path than they would if there were no sign. Besides actually altering a setting, one can also use it in a new way, which thereby changes others' view of what the setting "is" and what can be done there. When a group performs a street play on the previously unused side steps of a city hall building, they call attention to that spot as an effective natural stage set (see photo on p. 8).

THE IMPACT OF COLLECTIONS OF PEOPLE

People usually have a more noticeable impact on settings when they are aggregated in groups, organizations, or collectives (when large numbers of people are in the same location but are not really members of a group or system and have in common only their location at the moment). Collections of people influence settings in two main ways: by their numbers, and by group behavior patterns.

The Effects of Numbers

When a setting regularly contains large numbers of people, such as New York's Time Square area, or Fisherman's Wharf in San Francisco (see photo on p. 103), spirit of place is partly shaped by the actual space the people occupy. They are mobile physical features of the setting and must always be dealt with. They provide (and block) views, present obstacles to movement, offer visual interest in terms of changing scenes, and so on (see photo on p. 4). Shopping in a giant suburban mall on a busy Saturday is an experience more related to dealing with other shoppers than dealing with merchandise.

There are certain physical features that often determine how big a factor the presence of people will be. The most obvious of these is weather: when mild it encourages outdoor activities (see photo on p. 174), and when harsh it encourages people to seek the indoors (see photo on p. 13). In England, the fair-weather impact of tourists on Cornwall is a classic example:

> Another trouble is that the rest of the country seems to take note of Cornwall only in the summer months when there are holidays to be spent. This is not the best time of the year to sample any place, certainly not a place as cluttered with visitors as the Duchy is then. . . . There is a distinct danger here of killing the goose that lays the golden egg, as the County Council is well aware. The whole point of taking holidays in Cornwall, to get away from high-density living to beautiful surroundings, would rapidly be lost if the spread of chalets, tents and caravans were allowed to go much further.
>
> (Geoffrey Moorehouse, *The Other England: Britain in the Sixties*)

For a person in a setting, then, the weather is a double factor: it affects immediate physical feel and look (the Chicago lakefront is quite different in lazy August sun than in a windy December storm), and it affects distribution and patterns of people (being in San Francisco's Union Square is one social experience on a mild May morning and quite another on a raw November day).

This effect also suggests that the weather and other factors encourage nonrandom use of wilderness areas. I am reluctantly supportive of experimental reservation systems for United States National Parks. Even though having to reserve space for hiking or camping is poor in terms of spontaneous place experiences, it may well be necessary if we are to be able to have any wilderness experiences at all. It is similar to going to the Boston Symphony (tickets to which are scarce)—it would be nice to go on the spur of the moment, but if you want to hear the Symphony you actually have to plan quite far ahead.

As populations grow and natural resources shrink, there is an increasing interest in the effects of crowding and overcrowding, where relatively large numbers of people are using a limited space or setting. Some of these effects include competition for scarce resources, physiological and emotional stress, excitement and stimulation, and heavy wear on the physical features of the setting itself. Many of the commonly accepted effects of crowding are really the effects of high density, which may be positive or negative, depending on the structure of the setting and the social context (such as the extent to which the people share similar values).[1] Density plus scarce resources leads to a feeling of being crowded, whereas density plus sufficient resources tends to generate vitality and excitement. This helps to explain how residents can love Hong Kong, an area with a higher absolute density of people than many depressing urban slums in the United States, and yet also having water, hills, and a great variety of sights and activities.

There are other ways in which the presence of people can provide a positive spirit of place. One is the opportunities for mutual help a group can provide, as did the Mormons who settled the state of Utah. Their collaborative social norms plus their concentrated settlements (rather than spreading out on isolated farms) created a supportive social context in a harsh, challenging physical environment.

People in numbers also may provide a sense of security in a setting against the threats of other human beings, as when many walkers on city streets provide observers who deter muggers and other criminals. Again, the effectiveness of people as security depends also on the accepted norms, such as whether one should intercede when another person is in trouble.

Finally, the presence of people in large numbers often plays the important function of filling out the setting, providing important background that makes the setting feel just right for its time and use. A large crowd at a football game makes for a different and more festive event than stands that are three-quarters empty. In the heyday of the Hollywood movie industry, this function of people as props for the scenes was recognized as critical to the atmosphere of films. The "extras" were really "necessaries" as far as total mood was concerned.

The value of collections of people in creating festive moods should be emphasized. There are certain settings such as Boston's Charles River

Esplanade on a summer's evening, or San Francisco's Ghirardelli Square (see photo on p. 191) that become special places when they are filled out with people celebrating or just relaxing in a loose, friendly manner. I believe that unplanned, "natural festivals" are prime ingredients in the spirit of place of any good city; when these occur less and less frequently, one can almost feel the city decaying and dying. This is also a circular process: as residents sense the city becoming less safe or enjoyable, they move out, or choose to relax and play elsewhere, which further reduces the quality of enjoyment and leads to still fewer people using the city for natural festivals.

THE IMPACT OF PEOPLE'S TYPES AND STYLES

In addition to numbers, the kinds of people who inhabit or frequent a particular setting influence its spirit of place. The more consistently a type is found in a location the stronger the spirit of place.

A classic example is the selection processes that led to a special social climate on the island of Capri:

> Thus was founded the modern legend of Capri, but it reached its heady climax after the First World War, when the island became, above all else, a place of voluntary exile for hedonists. . . . Umberto II of Italy loved the place, and regularly moved there with his entire court. Queen Victoria of Sweden was a frequent visitor. The English aristocracy adopted the island, the grand white yachts of Empire lay frequently off the little harbour and one indomitable peer, for a substantial wager, walked stark naked from Capri to Anacapri. . . .
>
> And to capture this transient scene, to immortalize it as few pleasure havens have ever been saved from oblivion, a whole pack of writers fell upon the island—attended, as always, by those miscellaneous originals, charlatans, and dilettantes who cling to the coattails of art.
>
> (James Morris, *Places*)

This example is not meant to imply that self-selection always leads to a good or enjoyable atmosphere (that depends on one's values), only that it creates a strong identity for certain settings. The process is almost always a mixture of physical and social factors; the European spa of Baden-Baden was first popular because of its natural baths, before its royal clientele became the main drawing card. Capri has often been called the most beautiful spot in the world, and was a natural magnet for people who had the luxury of choosing where to be. Once a critical mass of wealthy and literary types gathered, the draw of the place was both physical and social. Similarly, the SoHo district in New York City attracted artists because of its physical features: good, affordable work spaces in factories and warehouses, a human scale for streets and buildings, and a nice ambience with its many castiron building fronts. Once a sufficient number of similar people had moved their homes, studios, and galleries there, the spirit of place became a sociophysical one, with the artistic atmosphere dominating.

The feel of an area is communicated by the messages displayed for its users, who in turn give it a still stronger identity by frequenting it.

Besides the types of people who use them, the atmosphere of a setting can be enhanced if there are narrowly focused activities occurring in them. A prime example is the city rooms of most large metropolitan newspapers. The combination of high density, focused and (sometimes) controlled panic, atmosphere of purpose and deadlines, and clatter of typewriters and voices all combine to create a special spirit of place. In discussing such a city room with one managing editor, I suggested that they could reorganize so that people's space did not overlap so much. He smiled and said that the whole point of the setting was to support and promote both competition and the swift interaction of people and functions that produces a live daily newspaper—so why would they want to "neaten it up?" I saw his point.

DOERS AND WATCHERS

There is another interesting distinction that can be made among types of users who provide a strong spirit of place. Some settings are used actively by "doers," and others are used passively by "watchers" or spectators. Some of the settings with the richest spirit are those that provide good opportunities for both, such as Italian towns where strolling at dusk and sitting by watching people strolling are both easy to do and supported by social norms. Settings that provide facilities for visible activities such as skating, basketball, tennis, football, chess, and speech-making, together with space for watchers, provide a focus for participants and spectators. Both provide atmosphere to the setting, and it would not be the same if either group was missing. Readers who have been to the skating rink at Rockefeller Center in New York in winter will immediately be able to imagine how incomplete that setting would be without one or the other.

Doers and watchers: the Galleria skating rink in Houston.

Doers and watchers: lunchtime basketball in Lincoln's Inn Fields, London.

Physical location is a big factor in success. This is why Rockefeller Center has such a strong atmosphere and festive spirit: it is in a central location in midtown Manhattan, with an enormous number of pedestrians passing through it each day. Many of them stop to relax and watch the skaters; some remain for 30 minutes, others for only 30 seconds, but the option is there because the rink is located on the way to and from so many other areas in Manhattan. This natural flow of audience material is contrasted with many suburban rinks that are unlikely to attract casual watchers as they are enclosed as well as located in areas that are not central and that are generally only reached by automobile—not encouraging for spontaneous spectators.

THE IMPACT OF SOCIAL CLIMATE

Social climate refers to the systems of rules, norms, values, expectations, and other factors that provide the guidelines, supports, and constraints for how people relate to each other in a given setting. Social climate has obviously been present in the previous examples, as it usually means the "feel" of a social setting, but I want to consider two more specific examples here: neighborhoods and other organizations with a tangible climate.

Neighborhoods

It is obvious that neighborhoods are defined by both social and physical features: the types of people who live in a given area, their common values, activities, and approaches to problems, and usually some kinds of physical boundaries (gates, walls, heavily traveled streets, industrial buildings) that mark the neighborhood's end and the beginning of somewhere else. As we

An area where the residents even make their culture felt on the hamburger stands: a clearly demarcated entrance to San Francisco's Chinatown.

WHAT SETTING BRINGS TO PLACE

describe in the chapter on perception, insiders experience a neighborhood differently, with greater awareness of certain features than visitors have. Residents are more aware of the social norms, and of the potential resources for support the neighbors represent, while visitors notice features different than those that prevail in their own areas. For visitors to Boston's Italian-American North End, a strong sense of place is experienced if they are aware of the human scale of the streets, the Italian shops that are not found in many parts of the United States, and the social climate as reflected by the large numbers of people who use the streets and alleys as extensions of their houses and apartments (see photo on p. 14). In a similar manner, the wide streets, lovely garden squares, and imposing cream-colored mansion terraces of an upper-class London neighborhood such as Knightsbridge communicates one spirit (home, tradition, security, good taste) to residents and another (elegance, wealth, possibly sterility and lack of human interaction) to visitors.

Organizational Climate

Organizational climate has also been used to describe social contributions to a spirit of place. Many organizations impart a distinct feel or atmosphere to those who work in them: warm or cold, tight or loose, exciting or dull, energized or lethargic, predictable or unpredictable, and so on. Physical features help to create this climate, but a good portion of it is maintained by the ways that the social system impacts on people with its norms, rules, policies, expectations, and management style.[2]

Sometimes the physical and social spirits clash, as when rigid rules block the creation of settings that would be well matched to users' needs, as one disillusioned designer discovered:

> We designed an elementary school in a place where the temperature only rose above 80 degrees (Fahrenheit) during the two months of the year when the school was not open. Yet the state administrators of education said that the school had to have air conditioning; that the cost of air conditioning was worth the price of one extra classroom. We spent more time getting the air conditioning out of the plans than we did designing the whole school. The solution would not have worked without the extra classroom and the teachers, pupils, and parents, all acknowledged air conditioning to be absurd.
>
> (Walter Kleeman, "Whatever Happened to Sam Sloan?" *The Designer*, November 1976)

In general, however, most organizations do generate a strong spirit of place through both their formal and informal rules, and the physical symbols of climate they create or acquire. Building and furniture styles, art and other decorative elements, layouts of work places, signs and personal memorabilia all provide symbolic messages both to insiders and outsiders about the kind of organization it is and the setting it offers employees.

Socio-legal and physical features in a city combine to set a climate for pedestrians: Boston says "don't be here," and London has a public "street" that passes right through a building and invites use.

In case it has not yet become obvious, my personal biases lie with physical and social spirits of place that free people rather than bind them; that allow exploration and some risk-taking rather than requiring strict adherence to a predetermined set of behaviors; and that allow some options about when and how a setting can be used. These are all outcomes of a rich sociophysical spirit of place, and the presence of people in varying mixes of residents and visitors, doers and watchers, members and guests, helps create this type of setting.

NOTES

1. Charles Mercer, *Living in Cities,* Harmondsworth, Middlesex: Penguin Books, 1975, Chapter 8.
2. For an exploration of both physical and social organizational climate see Fritz Steele and Stephen Jenks, *The Feel of the Work Place: Understanding and Improving Organizational Climate* (Reading, Mass.: Addison-Wesley Publishing Co., 1977).

8   The Special Spirit of Mystery

A special quality exuded by some settings is a spirit of mystery. These settings have the ability to elicit consistent reactions: awe, surprise, wonder, dread, or vague uneasiness, all of which generate a strong sense of place. Although there has been a tendency to take this experience of mystery as something unknowable that just "is," there are some interesting, identifiable factors that contribute to it: physical features of the setting, and cultural themes created by the social context of the setting.

PHYSICAL FEATURES

Potent Elements

One type of mystery setting has some potent topographical features that jar an observer or user; a person must somehow deal with the setting, because it cannot be ignored or treated as just anyplace. Such a setting is the Devil's Tower area of South Dakota:

A dark mist lay over the Black Hills, and the land was like iron. At the top of a ridge, I caught sight of Devil's Tower—the upper-most extremity of it like a file's end on the gray sky. . . . It stands in motion like certain timeless trees that aspire too much into the sky, and imposes an illusion on the land. There are things in nature which engender an awful quiet in the heart of man; Devil's Tower is one of them. Man must account for it. He must never fail to explain such a thing to himself, or else he is estranged forever from the universe.

(N. Scott Momaday, *House Made of Dawn*)

Striking geographic features that contrast markedly with their surroundings spark questions in those who see and use them: How did this place come to be this way? What has gone on here? What is different about it from other places? What does it mean for me? What should I do to remain in the good graces of such a powerful setting? High mountains that contrast with their surrounding plains generate such a mood, as they are almost always visible and therefore somewhere in people's awareness. Even when they are covered by clouds and mists, their presence is a strong force.

This is an example of the sharp contrast of adjacent features we described in Chapter 6. Such contrasts as deserts and lush oases, plains and abrupt gorges or mountains are often associated with feelings of mystery. Examples are quite abundant: the Ngorongoro Crater in Africa, the Grand Canyon in the United States, Malham Cove in England's Yorkshire dales, or the Black Canyon of the Gunnison River in Colorado. The ability of both mountains and gorges to generate a sense of mystery for first-time viewers is enhanced if these spots have been prominent in stories and legends, so that people connect the immediate scene with some history—fact or fiction.

Fog and mist have always lent an air of mystery to settings, such as this rugged California coastline.

WHAT SETTING BRINGS TO PLACE

Odd Combinations of Features

Sometimes mystery is generated not by the grand contrast of the setting, but by its odd combinations of features, which raise questions about one's habitual ways of seeing things. In some cases, the setting is surprising enough consciously to challenge assumptions, as when a traveler first came upon the Eskimos' stone men piled in the Barrens of the Arctic:

> We looked out over a dead land—but not a deserted one, for our eyes quickly discovered the shapes of men standing in monumental immobility on every side of us.
>
> They were men, but men of stone! Insensate little pillars of flat rocks piled precariously atop each other, they stood on every hill, by every lake and river, as they have stood throughout the long ages of the people who created them and called them *Inukok* (semblance of men). They are such puny monuments, these lone inhabitants of emptiness, it seems inevitable that they must topple into the anonymity of the rock slopes from which they sprang. And yet they will not fall.
>
> (Farley Mowat, *People of the Deer*)

It is possible that chance events can sometimes generate this feeling of mystery through odd combinations. Seeing a whole herd of cows facing the same direction on a hillside can make an impression, as can the moment on a busy downtown street when a particular block has no pedestrians at all and the adjacent ones are crowded. Such moments have no particular meaning except as statistical oddities, and yet one wonders . . .

Unknown Contents

Perhaps the most basic definition of mysterious is "being unknown," so that settings whose qualities and features are unknown or uncertain would be particularly likely to spark a mood of mystery.

As we might expect, inaccessibility plays a major role in maintaining an unknown quantity. The more difficult it is physically to reach a particular site, the more likely that it will remain unknown to most people, and the more people's images of the setting will be projected from inside themselves onto the reports from those few who have actually been there. The range and behavior of the Abominable Snowman in the Himalayas retains a spirit of mystery because of the area's inaccessibility and harsh weather patterns. The Snowman would not long serve as a target for projections and fantasies if its habitat were Los Angeles or Kansas City.

Many recent conservation writers have raised questions about the advisability of big road-building programs for United States wilderness areas under the banner of "improvements":

> The Developers insist that the parks must be made fully accessible not only to people but also to their machines, that is, to automobiles, motorboats, etc. The Preservers argue, in principle at least, that wilderness and motors are incompatible and that the former can best be experienced, understood, and enjoyed when

machines are left behind where they belong—on the superhighways and in the parking lots, on the reservoirs and in the marinas.

(Edward Abbey, *Desert Solitaire*)

In the terms of this chapter, when a road allows a person to drive right to some area of particular grandeur or challenge, the sequence of experiences (seeking, struggling, anticipation, arrival) has been watered down, and the mystery has been lost. This may be an improvement in terms of the principle of least effort, but not in terms of the quality of the experience. Whatever mystery and threat one may feel when standing on the edge of a chasm that must be crossed with a pack on one's back, it is totally lost when viewing the same sight from the driver's seat of a 1977 Ford Gran Torino. Aesthetic, perhaps, but mysterious only if one has some question about how well the car's brakes will function on the way down. If a setting is totally known in all its features, we gain an experience of security, comfort, or ease, but we lose one of special accomplishment, for it is partly the challenge of the unpredictable aspects that serves to energize us, to make us more attuned to subtleties in the setting, and generally to stimulate a richer experience of place.

The other main experience of mystery in unknown settings is not caused by physical inaccessibility, but by an air of our inability to reach through to the forces in the site that are spiritually inaccessible, as in this example of

Coming upon this church shell for the first time makes one wonder how it came to be here, on such a distinctive site.

Carlos Castaneda's experience at the Mexican desert home of Yaqui sorcerer don Juan:

> There was something eerie about don Juan's house. For a moment I thought he was hiding somewhere around the place to scare me. I called out to him and then gathered enough nerve to walk inside. . . . But for the first time in my years of associating with don Juan I was afraid to stay alone in his house. I felt a presence, as if someone invisible was there with me. I remembered then that years before I had had the same vague feeling that something unknown was prowling around me when I was alone. I jumped to my feet and ran out of the house.
>
> (Carlos Castaneda, *A Separate Reality*)

In American culture, people experience this in several familiar kinds of settings, such as graveyards, older churches, and some houses that seem to have a history that has left them with an aura of mystery, but nothing tangible to account for it (see photos on p. 129 and p. 130). Many recent thriller movies, such as "The Amityville Horror," have been based on this effect, although for the sake of drama, the results are quite a bit more drastic than they usually are for most of us in such settings. The typical experience is a feeling of uneasiness, excitement, and conflicting desires to learn more about the setting and to get out of it as soon as possible.

CULTURAL AND SOCIAL FACTORS IN MYSTERIOUS SETTINGS

Sacred Status

Groups and cultures endow certain sites with the status of being sacred, that is, serving as a link between earth and heaven, mortality and immortality, or the mundane affairs of humans and the mighty concerns of the gods. This designation increases the mood of mystery associated with the setting, as it implies that there are superhuman forces and purposes at work there. For example, there is a small hot spring in Arizona's Grand Canyon the Hopi Indians call a Sipapu—"the place where their primeval ancestors emerged from the earth."[1] They experience that spring as more charged with mystery than if they did not know that it was sacred. (There may, however, be enough of a "feel" to the place that people may sense it as different without knowing this legend.)

Settings take on sacred aspects as a result of both real and mythical events that are associated with them, including famous battles, holy persons' experiences, calamitous events, and special visions or visitations. Once these associations are built up, they become real for future visitors by conjuring up feelings of awe and mystery. This spirit is therefore mainly the result of human history and culture; but it generally is reinforced by the specific physical features, such as the previously mentioned Devil's Tower's contrast with its surroundings, which made it more likely that this particular setting, rather than others would be deemed sacred.

Known History

If a setting is known to have a particularly interesting or compelling history, traces of that history can generate a certain spirit of mystery. Particularly potent settings of this type are sites previously inhabited by human beings but no longer settled, such as the abandoned cliff-dwellings of Canyon de Chelly in Arizona:

> There is—I almost hate to use the term, but I must—there is a haunting quality to the sound of the wind here, aided by the echoes and acoustics of soaring cliffs, dead-end canyons, curving alcoves. There is an eeriness even now in broad daylight, that brings reminiscences of childhood fears of haunted houses and the unknown darkness. Sitting here amid ruins of an ancient structure built more than a thousand years ago, I sense ghosts all about me. With the first light of dawn, I begin hearing the distant murmur of voices from a village across the canyon: men calling to one another as they prepare to climb the steps carved into the cliff to tend the mesa-top fields of crops.
>
> (Boyd Norton, *Rivers of the Rockies*)

I have had similar fantasies of past communal life while wandering among the abandoned English tin mines in Yorkshire's Swaledale, and I know that a little knowledge of the area's history is all it takes to send me back in time when I am there.

Unknown History

Perhaps even more stimulating than commonly known historic settings are those whose contents are known but whose history of human influence has somehow not been recorded or otherwise maintained: the mystery is not what is there, but how it got that way. A familiar example is Stonehenge on England's Salisbury plain, and the plethora of theories about the site's origins and functions have not fundamentally reduced the unmistakable mood of mystery that hangs over it like a cloak (especially if one is lucky enough to see it when there are not many other visitors about).[2]

Human beings seem to be drawn particularly to the test of explaining the actions and impact of much earlier generations (e.g., how some of the huge Stonehenge monoliths were raised without modern technical devices; built-up earthworks is the currently accepted answer), and why they did it. Our greatest mysteries are about human behavior, and therefore about those sites that were strongly influenced by our ancestors in what to us are unusual or unpredictable ways.

(This type of mystery has filled many volumes, and it is therefore much too broad to cover here. I would suggest, however, that the interested reader see the DeCamps' fascinating descriptions of the structure and legends of a number of such mysterious man-made settings all over the world, including

The Wupatki monument in northern Arizona holds a strong air of mystery because we still do not know why the residents abandoned it many centuries ago.

the Pyramid Hill, Egypt; Stonehenge, U.K.; Tintagel Castle, U.K.; Angkor, Thailand; Zimbabwe, Southern Africa; Rapa Nui, Easter Island; and Machu Picchu, Peru.[3])

Pure Atmosphere

All of these factors can be contributors to a spirit of mystery in a particular setting, and yet, when all are considered, there are settings in which there remains an undivinable something, a mysterious quality that may be hard to analyze but is very real. It is hard to cite specific sites, as they would generally only have meaning for someone who had been there. I have a friend who remembers growing up near a wooded area that had a little mossy dell in the middle of it that used to make everyone who went there shiver with unease, adults and children alike. As neither I nor my readers have been there, it is hard for us to draw any conclusions about it.

What we can draw as an inference is that there clearly are such places in everyone's life. They may be famous ones such as the Island of Iona in the Irish Sea, or totally anonymous ones such as the dell just mentioned, or even a place I remember in a midwestern town where two streets joined in such a way that almost everyone who passed through felt in a vague way that something there was trying to tell them something. The anonymous place is not famous, because people don't think to tell one another about their feelings there, or to write plays and novels about it. The atmosphere makes it nonetheless mysterious, and therefore stimulating.

RESULTS OF THE SPIRIT OF MYSTERY

In closing this chapter, I will briefly review some of the main consequences of experiencing settings with a spirit of mystery.

Triggering Fantasies   Mystery-laden sites spark images, associations, fantasies, and scenarios, all of which are likely to contribute to a richer experience of place (as will be described in Chapter 14).

Feelings of Threat   The mysterious mood, especially when generated by a sense of unknown, can be threatening and can be taken as a signal of potential danger.

Cosmic Thoughts   For several of the examples in this and earlier chapters, the atmosphere of mystery has stimulated people to think beyond the immediate situation about much larger issues, including the basic mysteries of life itself. If this happens with enough regularity in a particular setting it usually becomes known as an appropriate site for a religious retreat or pilgrimage by people seeking new answers to their old questions about the world and their places in it.

A little paint trickery on the end wall is just enough to start passersby wondering about this Cambridge building.

WHAT SETTING BRINGS TO PLACE

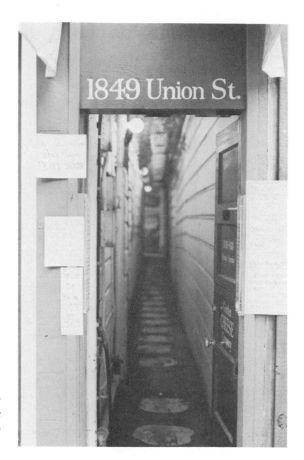

This entrance to a San Francisco restaurant must generate a sense of mystery, at least to first-time patrons.

Stimulation   Besides being threatening or uplifting, a mysterious setting can serve simply as an energizer, a stimulator of awareness, attention, interest, and action. This can provide rich experiences that break up the regular rhythm of our lives and provide changes of pace. I believe that people crave stimulation, and that even threatening places are preferable occasionally to being always in predictable, totally known surroundings that require no new perceptions or interpretations.

Consistent Effects on Relationships

Although not mentioned specifically in the above examples, a mystery setting may sometimes be identified by its consistent impact on the relations between users. A house in the countryside outside Boston is reputed to have "caused" the break-up of four consecutive couples who lived in it (although there could also be some connection between having a shaky marriage and choosing to live in the house in the first place). The setting's mood of mystery, in other words, may be communicated by its strange impact rather than just by its direct atmosphere.

Scale, light, and shadow create a strong mood in this old shopping street in London.

Two final thoughts should be added. One is that these outcomes can be enhanced for people who think of the property of mystery in settings as providing opportunities for interesting experiences or stimulation. This suggests that a good strategy if one is feeling boxed-in or circumscribed by day-to-day matters would be to seek out some settings with mystery in their atmosphere, and use them as a stimulus to get out of the rut. The second point is that many settings that we take for granted have the potential for stimulating questions, fantasies, and odd moods in us if we start to look at their details more closely, or approach them with more curiosity about how they got the way they are. Many settings we dismiss as mundane are rich with potential, but our expectations of them are ordinary, and therefore our experiences are as well.

NOTES

1. Colin Fletcher, *The Man Who Walked Through Time*, New York: Alfred A. Knopf, 1968.
2. This is now less of a problem, as the immediate Stonehenge area has been closed to visitors, due to the rapid destruction of the site the volume of pedestrians was causing. Viewing Stonehenge from a distance will probably increase its impact as a mystery setting.

WHAT SETTING BRINGS TO PLACE

9

It Looks Lived-In: The Spirit of Personal Places

There is a special spirit of place that is likely to be familiar to most readers, although they may not have thought much about how it is caused. This is the spirit of personal place: the feel of a setting that is intimately associated with a particular person or group, so that everybody thinks of it as such. We might call this type of setting a true "place," as it has a strong identity that communicates the same messages to different users about the personality and life style of the owner.

TWO EXAMPLES

Here are two examples, one fictional and one a real setting. First, Lady Marchmain's sitting room:

> This room was all her own; she had taken it for herself and changed it so that, entering, one seemed to be in another house. She had lowered the ceiling and the elaborate cornice which, in one form or another, graced every room, was lost to view; the walls, one panelled in brocade, were stripped and washed blue and spotted with innumerable little water-colors of fond association; the air was

83

sweet with the fresh scent of flowers and musk potpourri; her library in soft leather covers, well-read works of poetry and piety, filled a small rosewood bookcase, the chimneypiece was covered with small personal treasures—an ivory Madonna, a plaster St. Joseph, posthumous miniatures of her three soldier brothers. When Sebastian and I lived alone at Brideshead during that brilliant August we had kept out of his mother's room.

(Evelyn Waugh, *Brideshead Revisited*)

These are excerpts from a description of humorist Robert Benchley's famous living quarters in New York's Royalton Hotel:

Bookcases were installed on all four walls, and three pictures of Queen Victoria, one of them framed in red velvet, were hung between the windows. He covered the walls with every kind of picture he could find, and as time passed, his family and friends contributed enough so that there was practically no bare space showing.

. . . Between the drape-covered windows was a bookcase which stood about chest-high, and this was the cause of the collection that later all but got out of hand, and made the room the cleaning-woman's hell that it was. Robert wanted some knickknacks to put on top of this bookcase, he started it with miniature geese, globes that made snow storms when shaken and gruesome little figures carved out of roots. He invited contributions from his friends, and suddenly there was a new game, called Dig it Up, Dust It Off and Give it to Benchley. . . . In almost no time, the bookcase was overflowing onto the tables and desks, and Robert found himself swamped with, as he described it, "old busts of Sir Walter Scott, four-foot statues of men whose shirt fronts lit up when attached to an electric connection, stuffed owls, and fox terriers that had lain too long at the taxidermists."

. . . Between the table and the couch was a red chair with white antimacassars that were always coming unpinned, and in front of the chair was a card table on which he read the papers and played solitaire. The chair was just low enough and comfortable enough so that it was hard to get out of, and he sometimes spent most of his day there.

He did his writing on a portable typewriter table, which was small and low and could be pushed out of the way when anything more important came up.

. . . To a newcomer, the room had a baffling, almost overwhelming effect. There was too much to be taken in all at once, and yet of the disorder there came a kind of relaxing sense of order, because there was no emphasis on any particular item. The first time Noel Coward visited the room, he came in, looked quickly about him, and said "So *this* is your little rose bower . . . I must say, it looks lived in."

(Nathaniel Benchley, *Robert Benchley*)

I can only add that the description here does not capture more than a small portion of the accumulation in Benchley's place.

What are the qualities that create a spirit or personal place? The answer is as long and varied as human history, but we can select some of the more frequent features, using the two descriptions as examples. Not all are found in all personal places, of course, but are frequently associated with them.

Territory   The place is seen as the territory or domain of the prime person, with two effects: (1) others tend to defer to that person and to limit their behavior (as with Lady Marchmain's sitting room) when in it; and (2) the owner behaves differently in home territory, exhibiting a confidence that signals "this is mine" to others. For example, therapists have found that client families often behave much more competently and show greater strength in sessions held in their own homes than they do meeting in the therapist's office. This is similar to animals behaving more confidently and aggressively in their home territory.

Tinkering and Products   The setting was usually built or altered by the prime person who has changed it somehow and left a mark on it, as in Lady Marchmain's impact on the design of her sitting room, or Benchley's "decoration" of his space. The person may have supervised the changes, or even have done the work, in which case the place holds even more meaning and attachment for the owner.

Special Furniture   As tools for stable living patterns, pieces of furniture often become central anchor points for personal places, such as Benchley's red chair and deliberately flimsy work table. In fact, in households or institutions where scarce resources do not allow whole rooms for personal places, people often lay claim to a particular chair or desk that becomes their special spot, that is so recognized by others who may use it when it is free, but is deferred to the "owner" when there is a conflict.

Vita Sackville-West's tower room at Sissinghurst Castle, Kent.

(Reproduced by permission of Nigel Nicolson)

IT LOOKS LIVED-IN: THE SPIRIT OF PERSONAL PLACES

Visible Themes   The personal place often contains visual displays that indicate the person's interests, values, and preferred activities. If one is able to recognize them, dominant themes are there to be observed, such as Lady Marchmain's well-read books of poetry and religion, and her ceramic Madonnas; Benchley's (admittedly not prominent) writing table plus bound volumes of both *Life* and *The New Yorker* (for which he wrote) lying about in his room; and the makeshift cat toys (bottle caps, wine corks, bells) my wife and I leave lying about for the cats in our home, which are often taken as random rubbish by our visitors.

Three personal workplaces: desks of three university roles: president, custodian, and design professors (a shared place).

(Photographs by Mark Ellis, © Yale Alumni Magazine)

WHAT SETTING BRINGS TO PLACE

Traces of Friends   People's identities are always shaped to some extent by the nature and influence of their close friends and relatives. Personal places can reflect ties to significant people such as the morass of artifacts from Benchley's friends, or Lady Marchmain's pictures of her brothers.

Boundaries   The most potent personal places usually have distinct boundaries of some sort, so that there is a clear line between here (the personal place) and not here (other settings). Lady Marchmain's sitting room was differentiated from any other setting in the house, and visitors had to run a gauntlet of junk just to get into Benchley's rooms.

Two other elements of personal places are more conditional; they are present or not, depending on certain circumstances. One is the element of privacy, which we often associate with personal places, but which is not necessarily a feature of them. Privacy may be manifested by a strong visual boundary (such as walls); it may be demonstrated in an out-of-the-way spot; or it may be a particular location (corner, chair, section of grass) in a relatively public area, such as favorite benches for older citizens in their neighborhood parks. Benchley's apartment was dark and withdrawn, yet accessible because of his personality.

The second conditional quality is related; it concerns ownership. People sometimes own their places and sometimes they do not, however, so it is not a foolproof test of a personal place. (Lady Marchmain owned her place, while Benchley rented his.) For example, the tenant-caretaker of a Newport, R.I. mansion describes the setting as "my house," and identifies closely with it, even though he could never "own" it.[1] The reverse is also true: ownership by one person does not make a setting a personal place, that is, a person's place is not necessarily a personal place. That depends on whether it has the special qualities that have just been described.

EFFECTS OF PERSONAL PLACES

Given the fact that they exist, what is the value of personal places? Just as with other types of settings, personal places help to fulfill basic human needs, especially those of security, identity, social contact, and growth.

Shelter and Security

An obvious function of personal places is to provide a base for self-protection and security from the surrounding environment. Even relatively dehumanizing mental hospitals have "free places" where hospital inmates can withdraw from the usually constant surveillance of the hospital staff.

> Thus, underneath some of the buildings there was an old line of cart tracks once used for moving food from central kitchens; on the banks of this underground trench, patients had collected benches and chairs, and some patients sat out the day there, knowing that no attendant was likely to address them.
>
> (Erving Goffman, *Asylums*)

In homes, family members will establish claims to certain areas that are labeled as their domain (e.g., Mom in "her" kitchen, Dad in "his" workshop) and therefore serve as withdrawal areas as well as activity spaces. Families who live in cramped spaces and who do not develop these personal claims have higher levels of disruption and conflict than those who do.[2]

Sense of Identity

This is the function first used to define personal places. It is the communication of information about the prime person's identity to themselves and other people. For example, Sir John Soane's house in London (now a museum) served as his home, office, and gallery, and as such communicated strongly about both his work (architecture) and his interests (classical design, innovation, collecting as a leisure activity).

Office work areas often serve a similar function, with symbols of interests (family, hobbies, art, plants, and so on) mixed with more task-oriented items. We should keep in mind that in looking at a setting for clues about the person's identity, we have to know something about who made the choices. For example, many of the memorials set up for famous people reflect the arrangers' ideas of what their settings should have looked like, and bring together elements the owners never used. Thus what are created are rigged personal places.

A *real* personal workplace. Where does the person stop and his place begin?

WHAT SETTING BRINGS TO PLACE

Social Contact

Personal places are often organized to allow the owner to control contacts with other people. Here is a fine example from a novel about the publishing world:

> Bernard's desk was at right angles to the window. Behind it he had made a nest for himself, a refuge against the world, where he could recapture some vestiges of pre-natal irresponsibility. A broad parapet of books stretched across the top of the desk. Another similar but higher barrier ran along the ledge of the window. . . . The shelves of another bookcase at his back tipped forward waywardly as if at any moment they might void their contents on his head. His fourth and most vulnerable side was protected by newspapers thrown about on the floor in such quantities that they formed a sort of pyramid. When visitors ignored this barricade Bernard would point warningly to the ground as if these journals concealed chasms yawning in the floor.
>
> (Anthony Powell, *What's Become of Waring?*)

Although this is a fictional example, many real offices are arranged by their occupants to control the options and therefore the power of visitors to influence what happens there, as well as to maintain distance from visitors. I have also seen the opposite, where the placement of furniture and level of lighting encouraged a sense of intimacy.

Oscar Newman's research on crime and council housing design in New York City led him to recommend design configurations that would instill a sense of personal place identification in the residents, who would therefore feel responsible for controlling the intrusion and behavior of strangers. This is an example of personal place leading to control of contact, which in turn increases shelter and security for residents.[3]

Growth

Some people are able to use places as a stimulus to their own growth and development. One of the nicest examples I have found is pioneer psychologist Carl Jung's description of the development of his house (which he called the Tower) over many years and alterations:

> From the beginning I felt the Tower as in some way a place of maturation—a maternal womb or a maternal figure in which I could become what I was, what I am and will be. It gave me a feeling as if I were reborn in stone. It is thus a concretization of the individuation process, a memorial *aere perennius*. During the building work, of course, I never considered following the concrete needs of the moment. It might also be said that I built it in a kind of a dream. . . . Only afterward did I see how all the parts fitted together and that a meaningful form had resulted: a symbol of psychic wholeness.
>
> (C. G. Jung, *Memories, Dreams, Reflections*)

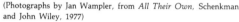

Two very personal places which show us all how little of our potential for real personalization we usually use.

(Photographs by Jan Wampler, from *All Their Own*, Schenkman and John Wiley, 1977)

This beautiful passage also suggests that in order to stimulate growth, a personal place generally must be dynamic, not static. One cannot expect to create it once and for all, perfectly, from the beginning. The freedom to tinker with it is essential to its value as an aid to growth, as it allows the person to test out or express the changes in themselves, and then help to stimulate the next set of changes.

Drawbacks

I must add that personal places do not always play positive functions for their owners; there can be costs involved that are the reverse of gains from positive functions. For instance, one's sense of security in a personal place can be a block to moving out and connecting with the surrounding environment of things and people, as in Alexander Solzhenitsyn's fictional description of Stalin's use of his study as a refuge from unknown threats:

> Stalin got up and walked the length of the small study, his favorite place for working at night. He went up to a little window that was glazed with two layers of yellowish bullet-proof glass divided by air under high pressure. Outside was a little, walled garden into which the gardener was admitted only in the mornings and then under guard.

WHAT SETTING BRINGS TO PLACE

. . . That half of the universe which was within him felt orderly and manage-able. It was the other half, so-called objective reality, which lurked out there in the mist. Here, within his armour-plated study, Stalin was not afraid of that other half. . . .

He himself had called space the basic condition for the existence of matter. Yet having made himself master of one sixth of the world's dry land, he had begun to fear space. What he liked about his study was its very lack of space.

(Alexander Solzhenitsyn, *The First Circle*)

A related drawback is that one can become so attached to one's personal place that it is difficult to move on to a new one, even when such a move would bring new ideas, feelings, and energy to the mover.

A third problem is that a place can become so personal that it becomes unusable by other people. Vita Sackville-West's sitting-room in the Tower at Sissinghurst was so steeped in her spirit that her son Nigel found it impossible to use it as his own after her death; he seemed almost to be taken over by her ghost.[4] (See photo on p. 85.)

SETTINGS THAT ARE NOT PERSONAL
PLACES

There are, of course, many settings that are not personal, for example, those areas that are owned, influenced, and used jointly by numbers of people. They are not identified with any single owner, and provide the large bulk of useful settings for our everyday lives. Many public spaces are nonpersonal, available to many types of people or groups.

The second type is the "no-person's place," the setting for which no one feels any responsibility or ownership (versus multiple ownership feelings). These settings have no character, are seldom influenced by anyone, are poorly maintained, and are avoided whenever possible. Organizations often create large expanses of no-person's land through rigid policies about employees not impressing personality on corridors, or other spaces not being owned by par-ticular work groups. Many public spaces take on this same dead quality, as no citizens feel any responsibility to enliven them or freedom to influence them.

I believe that there is something to be gained through creating personal places for ourselves, and through recognizing others' personal places more re-sponsively. This is one antidote to the trend toward larger and larger expanses of no-person's lands in our society.

N O T E S

1. Nick King, "He Lives Like a Vanderbilt," *Boston Globe*, Feb. 1, 1976.
2. See the research reported by Norman Ashcraft and Albert Scheflen, *People Space* (Garden City, N.Y.: Anchor Doubleday, 1976).
3. Oscar Newman, *Defensible Space*, New York: Collier Books, 1973.
4. Nigel Nicolson, *Portrait of a Marriage*, New York: Atheneum, 1973, p. 224.

PART FOUR

THE LONG-TERM IMPACT OF SPIRIT OF PLACE

10 Looking Down on the World

One of the most interesting and important aspects of the sense of place is its influence on our perceptions, attitudes, and likes and dislikes, if it is experienced over many years or during the formative years of childhood. The notion that there are long-term effects of settings is probably not new to most readers, but I believe that the cumulative effects of consistent place experiences cover more areas of perception and behavior than we usually recognize. We are aware of these effects in bits and pieces, if at all, and we seldom stop to ask what our favorite settings are doing or have done to shape the style and preferences we take for granted. To provide some clues for answering such a question, our discussion will explore long-term effects of both physical and social aspects of settings.

PHYSICAL FEATURES

As a common frame of reference for this and the two following chapters, I will begin by briefly describing a few of the main types of long-term impacts. Some are natural, while others are products of or alterations made by people.

Landscape   The most obvious (and often most potent) aspect of the physical setting is its geographic "feel": the nature of the land, sky, air, vegetation, and so on that form its structure. Living in the middle of the Arizona desert, with sand underfoot, intermittent cactus for vegetation, and few breaks in an otherwise flat horizon is a different experience from living on a farm in New Hampshire, with rolling hills and scattered rocks in the soil. Each of these is a far cry from the precipices and rarified air of the higher slopes of the Himalayas.

English writer Nan Fairbrother has distinguished several different categories for describing today's landscapes in Western societies: *built-up urban* (city centers), *green-urban* (city fringes), *rural* (mainly agricultural), and *man-made wild* (including commons, and county, state, or national parks). These reflect her notion that, especially in Britain and America, the press of population and recreation have created such conditions that no landscape is totally uninfluenced by humans.[1]

Climate and Weather   A second potent feature is the prevailing weather pattern: the mean temperature maximum and minimum, variation over the year, the amount of yearly precipitation and its distribution over the seasons, the degree of seasonal changes in temperature and moisture. It is obvious that an Eskimo living above the Arctic Circle must deal with weather as a key factor in survival, just as must a Bedouin who wanders the Arabian desert, or office workers in Wichita, Kansas who must deal with both some extremely cold spells in winter and some hot periods in the summer.

Dangers and Demands   Many geographic settings have special dangers, demands, or risks for people who live in them. These include threats from animal life, other hostile humans, potential natural disasters as exist in earthquake-prone areas, and man-caused effects such as high air pollution levels and overworked eroding hillsides or slag heaps produced in coal mining areas.

Enclosure   Locations vary both naturally and through human building as to the degree of enclosure they provide. By enclosure I mean having barriers and boundary markers such as hills, trees, buildings, and rivers that mark beginnings and ends of areas. A result is visibility—how far one can see before the line of sight is blocked.

Scale and Distances   Different settings have different scales, so that the same activity will require covering different distances depending on locale. One can drive for a hundred miles in parts of the state of Texas and see no basic change in the terrain, whereas in New Hampshire a 20-mile drive from the seacoast at Portsmouth brings one into the different world of the foothills of the White Mountains.

A traditional New England town common: growing up with a view of the world as crisp and sharp.

Building Styles, Symbolism, and Arrangements   The possible variations are obviously large, ranging from medieval walled towns in Europe that have been in place so long it seems they have grown out of the ground, to thatch compounds of the Ik mountain tribe in East Africa, where buildings are always meant to be temporary and symbolize the rapidly changing relationships in the Ik culture. In the United States today, one difference in settings that is likely to affect both preferences and perceptions is whether the region still contains a distinctive flavor or style of building, or has been homogenized by standard materials and methods so that it looks like anywhere (and nowhere).

Variety   This is really a pattern of other features; it is the extent to which the location provides a variety of new sights, smells, sounds, people passing through, changing structural patterns, all of which create a pattern of change (or stability) over time.

Technological Features   Roads and other modes of transport, mass media (newspapers, telephones, television, radio), climate control capabilities (inside structures), and so on interact with other features to determine or modulate the long-term impact of the setting. As a simple example, a physically isolated community that receives television generates a different sense of place than one that does not, and residents will develop different views of the world and their place in it.

LONG-TERM IMPACT

Given these dimensions in which settings can vary, how can we describe long-term impact on users, as shapers of behaviors, perceptions, attitudes, and skills? The following examples are organized by the nature of what is changed: perceptions, world view, levels of competence, preferences for types of settings, and so on.

Processes of Perception

There is a good deal of evidence that the nature of a person's early settings influences the development of basic perceptual processes. This is not just what images are seen at a particular moment (which of course should vary with what is there in the setting), but long-term patterns of *how* things are seen in new settings. For example, most readers of this book will take for granted the perception of distance and the use of perspective to estimate sizes of objects. But this process is developed in settings that both allow and require it. A differently structured environment does not produce the same mode of perception, as shown by the case of Pygmies growing up in the dense equatorial rain forest:

> As a human habitat the chief distinction of the rain forest environment lies in its all-enveloping nature. It is not differentiated as to sky and earth; there is no horizon; it lacks landmarks; it has no tree that exists in sharp isolation . . . there are no distant views.
>
> . . . An effect of the rainforest environment on perception is the curtailment of perspective. Anything that is seen is seen at close range.
>
> . . . Outside the rainforest the Pygmy is bewildered by distance, the lack of trees and the sharpness of relief. He seems incapable of reading the cues for perspective.
>
> (Yi-Fu Tuan, *Topophilia*)

Similar, although less pronounced, difficulties have been observed when inner-city children who have always lived in a dense environment first visit a rural setting with long views, a horizon, and large amounts of visible sky. We would also expect that people raised on the plains would have difficulty perceiving scales and angles in crowded cities, and they would have trouble orienting themselves in the absence of prominent features such as hills, that were always visible in their home settings. In this light, the stereotype of the first-time visitors to New York gawking at tall buildings takes on a different meaning: they are probably struck as much by the total effect, and with what they *can't* see (the skyline, hills, and so on) as by the sheer height of any single building.

World View

On a larger scale, strong physical settings can form a whole society's world view, that is, characteristic perception of the world and explanation of what they see. Settings dominated by natural topographic features encourage elaborate historical myths that incorporate those features. People who live in settings that regularly include natural forces (wind, sun, rain, animals, plants, changes of seasons) develop world views that give the forces a central role (such as ancient Egypt's view of the world with the Nile as the stabilizing element), while those who are seldom influenced by such factors (such as city dwellers) develop more political/economic/social explanations for events.

World view can also refer literally to how one sees the immediate physical world. One of my favorite examples is Edwin Way Teale's description of the Eskimo boy who had spent his whole life in the flat Arctic. At a Christmas party held on an upper floor of a building, he showed no interest in his presents, but rather spent his time at the window; looking down on the world was a fascinating new experience to be savored as long as possible.[2]

Competence and Skills

The physical setting often plays a major role in the development of competence and skills. For example, children in diverse settings develop a broader range of skills than do those in more restricted settings. Settings that are restricted, however, can encourage development of special skills needed for survival. People living in relatively harsh island environments become adept at perceiving changes in the sea and weather, as well as in dealing with the water.

Dealing with hills is just a fact of life if you grow up in San Francisco.

Physical endurance is also developed in groups living in demanding areas, such as the Tarahumara Indian tribe in the deep canyons area of north-central Mexico. The difficulties of movement there have developed them as a tribe of exceptional runners, with incredible endurance and speed on hills that many people find difficult even to walk up. Inner-city children develop another kind of movement skill—the ability to decipher and use urban transport systems—which is often an intimidating process for rural visitors. City children also learn other skills that are probably unnecessary for suburban people: where to find things quickly, how to get pleasure from less attractive (to downright ugly) settings, and how to tune out the noise and distraction of crowds in order to keep stress manageable. On the other hand, city children will usually be poorer than their country counterparts at sensing seasonal changes, reading terrain for clues about direction, and the like.

Personal Likes and Dislikes

One of the most prevalent assumptions about the long-term impact of place experience is that it affects people's individual characters: the style with which they do things, and preferences they have for different landscapes, buildings, and so on. This view was nicely expressed by a Scottish farmer who moved to the flat English county of Suffolk:

> The big skies leave the East Anglians empty. The skies are nothing. The horizons are too wide. There is nothing for a man to measure himself by here. In Scotland you have the hills, the mountains. They diminish a man. They make him think. . . . Because they are a flat-land creature there is a lack of imagination and excitement in the Suffolk character. You get very few real characters here.
>
> (Ronald Blythe, *Akenfield*)

Of course, the speaker is telling us not just about the Suffolk character, but about the impact of Scotland's hilly settings on his own preferences: "The skies are nothing. The horizons are too wide,"—each is a value judgment based on a feeling about what the "right" (or comfortable) landscape is like. The point is that individuals generally learn to love settings similar to or in contrast with, those in which they grew up.

Fundamentally, prolonged contact with a particular type of setting shapes people's preferences and style in several ways: one sees details and discovers qualities that are not noticed by short-term visitors; one has positive experiences that are then associated with the setting; one's basic activities are shaped by dealing with certain typical survival problems; and relaxation and play activities are influenced by the possibilities there (e.g., water plays a large part in recreation in Seattle, Washington, and a relatively small part in Dodge City, Kansas, so a preference for being around boats is much more likely to be developed in Seattle).

Creative Products

One of the most visible and lasting effects of settings is in shaping creative works of painters, writers, poets, and other artists. For painters, locale often determines both the types of works they do (landscape painters develop in settings of rich complexity or beauty) and their styles. It has been speculated that nineteenth century painter J.M.W. Turner's early life in London near the Thames River with its ever-changing light patterns was a significant factor in the development of his extraordinary power to perceive and portray light.

Writers' feelings, perceptions, and images are often a direct result of in-depth place experience. As one author described the process:

> I believe it is true, as William Carlos Williams said, that the world creates the mind. I think it is further true that the mind never loses the impression of the place that shaped it. Why else did Ibsen and Joyce, self-exiled from their native countries and hating them heartily, never write about anything but Norway and Ireland, and in the terms that their upbringing had made inescapable: Ibsen as a Northern Protestant moralist and Joyce as an inverted Jesuit?
>
> (Wallace Stegner, "The Writer's Sense of Place," *South Dakota Review*, Vol. 13, 1975)

There are many examples of American writers whose sense of place comes through as one of the main themes cutting across the plot lines of their individual novels: William Faulkner and his Mississippi county, Yawknapatawpha; Wright Morris and the central plains; John Updike and New England; and so on.

The long-term effect of settings on artists and writers is really a case of a more general phenomenon that happens to us all: the creation of a cache of images and stories that we then use as fantasy materials for the rest of our lives. A beautiful example was given by English poet Charles Causley on a BBC "Viewpoint" program: in his childhood, when he imagined Jesus giving the Sermon on the Mount, he always saw it occurring on the highest hill near his (Causley's) own home; when he thought about "hordes marching overland," he saw them coming over the brow of the hill he knew best. I suspect that most people do this to some degree, and some of us have indelible images as a result of living in potent settings that dominated (and continue to dominate) our fantasies, such as those just described in the preceding section of this book.

Effects of Built Settings

Although we have focused primarily on geographic features, a similar analysis could also be made of the long-term impact of strong settings created by people. An example is the structure of many newly built American housing development communities, where an automobile is required to reach almost any activity outside the home. It seems likely that there are cumulative but unrecognized effects from always using one's automobile: an unconscious assumption that events cannot happen spontaneously; a dependence that leads to near catatonia when the family auto is not working; and a tendency to spread oneself thin in terms of location of activity settings used (not to mention the cumulative amount of time spent in the car, reducing the need to walk for any great distance).

The impact of auto-dependent settings is an extension of a more general historical pattern: that of different modes of transport in shaping the experiences and opportunities for residents of different regions. In the nineteenth century, the coming of the railway line usually changed a small town's character very quickly, just as (less dramatically) a new interstate highway and series of exits can change a town's atmosphere today. The impact of an area on its inhabitants can also change dramatically when transport methods change. The introduction of the horse into the culture of the Plains Indians of the southwestern United States greatly increased their traveling ability, but also greatly expanded the territories needed to support them, thereby developing conflicts over territory among various tribes.[3]

SOCIAL FEATURES

Social features are also potent forces in shaping people's lives. This is a huge topic that will be limited to just one area here: ways in which these settings help create a sense of place and have lasting impact on their users. The focus is on the impact of relatively consistent *patterns* in the social climate in one's family, school, and social groupings, including: norms, values, characteristic patterns of interaction, expectations, and more formal laws and rules. These elements have a cumulative effect over time, as they are communicated through verbal statements, actions by others, and physical means such as signs and written messages.

Having Social Contacts

The long-term effects of social settings that encourage contacts with others tend to be positive (more growth, learning, enjoyment, good memories, and so forth) if there is adequate stimulation, but not too much (which can lead to an overload and possible withdrawal from interaction in defense against it).

For instance, it was found in Sweden that ". . . scores on a standard battery of intelligence tests are related to simple measures of access, based in turn, on population potential notions. Children in areas of high accessibility, literally in the swing of things, have a small but significant advantage on certain tests because of their locations in those intense nodes of human activity and communication."[4]

On interpersonal skills, television producer and commentator Sir Kenneth Clark wrote that lack of contacts with other children in his own youth kept him from developing facility for working in groups. On the other hand, he felt that the solitary social setting also produced a compensating gain:

> I have often been asked how I learnt the trick of talking to a television camera. I have no doubt at all that I did so on my long, solitary walks across the bog. People who are used to a companion require the stimulus of a listener.
>
> Actors are lost without an audience. But I formed the habit of soliloquy, and would even repeat out loud what I had learned on the preceding day very much as I did in "Civilisation."

(Kenneth Clark, *Another Part of the Wood*)

This passage exemplifies the general theme of this book, namely, that the sense of place and its impact are functions of both setting and person. Clark brought energy, curiosity, and previous exposures to the natural and artistic world to his solitary walks. For every person in a solitary setting who uses it well, however, there are undoubtedly several who do not become great soliloquizers as a result of the exposure. In other words, physical and social isolation did not *cause* Clark to develop this skill, but rather *aided* and *encouraged* its development when combined with his personal curiosity and tastes.

THE QUALITY OF SOCIAL CONTACTS

The impact of social settings obviously hinges not just on the sheer amount of contact, but also on its *quality* and the characteristics that make it distinctive.

Do people get to know one another fairly intimately, becoming familiar with personal details about many aspects of each other, or do they generally have only surface contacts that are ritualized or programmed by social conventions? For instance, children in small towns probably know more adults and learn to interact more easily with them than children in large cities do, even though, in absolute numbers, there are more adults in the city setting. The studies of Sidney Jourard have demonstrated that relationships that have a quality of self-disclosure breed a more healthy self-concept, increased self-understanding, and greater confidence in dealing with extreme problems and internal changes.[5]

Certain qualities of social settings have a consistently negative or energy-draining effect. Being limited to a social network that contains only similar types of people and that is rooted in one particular spot can lead to a minimum of knowledge about what exists in the rest of the world. People in physically isolated rural communities often develop a narrow range of knowledge, especially if they do not have access to television and other modern media. The same narrowness can be bred by being isolated in the middle of the city:

Teenagers and children in Harlem know very little of the outside world. Fantasy takes the place of reality. Teenagers pretend to knowledge that they do not really have, some modelling themselves after petty criminals, others after college students. . . . Children in Herbert Kohl's class had no idea that Columbia University existed, even though they could see it from their classroom window. Trips downtown beyond Harlem were bewildering experiences. When the youngsters emerged from the subway they had difficulty in connecting the spectacular Park Avenue of opulent apartment buildings, doormen, and clean sidewalks with the Park Avenue they knew: "Where are the tracks? Where are the ash cans?"

(Yi-Fu Tuan, *Topophilia*)

For city parents who want their children to have a wider, safer experience than many urban schools provide, there is a basic dilemma: going to private schools can produce intellectual stimulation, but it also places children in a selective social setting peopled with others like themselves. The trick is to provide a reasonably safe environment without making it over-protective and homogeneous at the same time.

THE COMBINATION OF PHYSICAL AND
SOCIAL FACTORS

The above example suggests an important closing point for this chapter: many of the long-term effects of the sense of place are the results of the combination of physical and social factors, which produces a different result than would either by itself. Sometimes one factor influences the other directly, as when social norms about avoiding physical closeness make the number of benches in a park inadequate for the number of potential users, so that many older people develop a pattern of staying indoors even though they would like to be outside.

In addition, a family home that receives fairly frequent guests from other parts of the country (or the world) would be a stimulator of knowledge and interests so that the children would learn to deal naturally and regularly with many different kinds of people, as opposed to just their own family and peers. This comes about through a necessary combination of a physical (the space and facilities to accomodate guests in one's home) and a social feature (having a network of friends at other locations, and particularly friends who tend to travel). This combination produces a richer, more expansive atmosphere than would either factor alone (facilities but no one to use them, or traveling friends but no place to put them). A third sociophysical factor is the location of the home: if it is in a highly desirable area to visit, the odds of friends dropping in are even higher, as some of my central London friends have discovered with both delight and some dismay (as another long-term impact may be to be drained of time and money by too many visitors).

We have already touched on one of the clearest instances of this combined effect in the area of human crowding. As recent reevaluations generally agree that crowding is a psychological experience (one kind of sense of place)

A person who grows up in the city knows how to take her havens where she finds them.

rather than an objective physical fact, the same density of people per given area will have different short- and long-term consequences depending on the learned preferences of the people, their needs at a particular time, the ways in which the space is organized (such as whether there are clear and controllable boundary mechanisms), and the social rules and norms that affect ability to control the amount of input received from one another.

NOTES

1. Nan Fairbrother, *New Lives, New Landscapes*, London: The Architectural Press, 1970, p. 247.
2. Edwin Way Teale, *A Naturalist Buys an Old Farm*, New York: Dodd Mead & Co., 1974, p. 289.
3. Norman Ashcraft and Albert Scheflen, *People Space*, Garden City, N.Y.: Anchor Books, 1976, p. 82.
4. Peter Gould and Rodney White, *Mental Maps*, Harmondsworth, Middlesex: Penguin Books, 1974, p. 143.
5. See Sidney Jourard, *The Transparent Self* (New York: Van Nostrand, 1964); and *Disclosing Man to Himself* (New York: Van Nostrand, 1968).

11 Occupations and Place Awareness: A Sixth Sense for Bones

One interesting long-term effect of settings is the development of an increased awareness of place and sense of place experiences. There are obviously settings that enhance this awareness, as well as ones that do nothing for it or even tend to dull it. A particularly relevant combined (social and physical) setting is a person's occupation. Some occupations have greater tendencies to develop an awareness of place experiences than others; thus people in certain occupations will be more aware of their place experiences than will members of other occupations. This influence is the complementary side of the question raised in Chapter 5, that is, whether there are place people who tend to gravitate to occupations that offer opportunities for satisfying place experiences.

We can begin with a rough distinction between two types of place occupations: (1) those in which place awareness is stimulated *because it is important to the tasks being done*, and therefore necessary for success; and (2) those occupations that produce place awareness as a *side benefit*, because of factors such as where and when the work is done. Examples of the former include travel writing, landscape painting, civil engineering, architecture, urban planning, farming, and caring for natural parks. Occupations in the latter category include construction work, transport, dance and choreography, and consultancy requiring travel.

Novelists and poets are an interesting mixed case, falling into both categories. Obviously, not all fiction is necessarily about settings, but writers who are able to use places well produce works that are both specific and universal. It has been said that mystery writer George Simenon will not set a story in a particular locale unless he has spent at least three days there "soaking up the atmosphere" before he begins.[1] Works that are "set" in places that communicate well to the reader often come alive in a way that unrooted pieces do not.

The more indirect benefit comes from writing as a process: by definition it involves a search for themes, patterns, action, events, and so on, that can be perceived, modified, and transmitted to others. The writer is bound to learn about settings and individual place experiences in the process of trying to produce a creative work.

CHARACTERISTICS OF PLACE
OCCUPATIONS

Some of the main characteristics that make an occupation more likely to generate place awareness in its members are: survival demands, task demands, opportunity structures, and patterns of experience.

Survival Demands

The most basic is the presence of regular danger or threat. People must be aware of their setting and learn how to evaluate its characteristics quickly to be ready for whatever threats it may contain. For instance, animals who survive by taking flight from danger (as opposed to fighting) seem always to know where they are in relation to safety; it is as if they keep in their field of vision a more or less updated map of the setting and themselves in it.[2] In a similar vein, there are occupations in which the practitioners survive by knowing when and how to take flight from threats to their physical safety.

Burglary is one that obviously springs to mind. A Boston police detective told me after I had been burglarized that my case was unusual, in that there was only one way into and out of my apartment. Most burglars are aware of entrances and exits and will generally not rob a home that has no alternate escape route. Years of practicing this trade and sizing the layouts of potential work areas would seem inevitably to lead to a heightened awareness of subtle place differences.

The military is another flight (as well as fight) occupation, and place awareness is such a strong component of military success that personnel generally receive a great deal of formal training in diagnosing terrain, evaluating gun positions, laying out possible lines of advance and retreat, reading maps, and the like. Many encounters in military history have gone to the side whose leaders had a keen sense of place and knew how to use it.

There is also a strong flight component in the lives of tramps who wander from town to town. Their lives depend on being able to find resources quickly and to avoid threatening situations (such as being arrested), thus we

The unique world of the professional fisherman: the sea presents special challenges.

(Courtesy of the Scottish Tourist Board)

would expect the more successful tramps to have a highly developed awareness of place. In fact, one study found that they have a strong knowledge of geography, and memory for significant details about different settings they had passed through.[3]

Task Demands

The second characteristic of place occupations is the extent to which the tasks themselves require the development of a strong awareness of place phenomena. As mentioned previously, place is central to the tasks of these occupations. The issue is still survival, but survival is *economic* rather than avoidance of physical harm, as those who are able to develop this awareness are more successful in the long run than those who are not.

Farming is an obvious place occupation whose success is heavily tied to awareness of settings. The farmer must understand the land, the weather, and their relationship to each other. For example, Ronald Blythe's classic study, *Akenfield, Portrait of an English Village*, contains a fine description of a retired military man turned farmer who was able to combine innovative methods with a good diagnosis of what his land could and could not do, and thereby succeeded with two small farms that had defeated many previous owners.[4]

Prospecting, in all its old and modern forms (for gold, silver, tin, oil, diamonds), is another occupation in which success is related to competence in dealing with settings and places. One of the most fascinating examples I have found of the prospector's sense of place is the development of the field of paleontology in the western United States in the nineteenth century. A number of people became famous for their ability to perceive settings that were likely to yield scientifically important fossils and bones. A legendary figure was John Bell Hatcher:

> Fellow bone hunters thought Hatcher had a sixth sense that led him to exposures of rock that contained fossil bone. His uncanny skill was based in part on a close study of rock that enabled him to imagine from the appearance of the rock the current flow in long-vanished streams, or to re-construct an eddy where a floating carcass might have come to rest.

> (Url Lanham, *The Bone Hunters*)

Hatcher no doubt brought natural ability to his profession, but I am sure that his years in the field contributed much to his awareness and sense of place. I also would guess that his ability carried over into assessing settings for other purposes as well, such as setting up camp sites so that they would not be washed away by flash floods.

A final example is the large category of design-related occupations, especially landscape architecture, urban planning, and interior design. Although

This architect/builder/teacher really experiences his sites because he has chosen to combine the three roles.

THE LONG-TERM IMPACT OF SPIRIT OF PLACE

designers vary tremendously in their ability to relate settings to the patterns and needs of human uses, if they are going to grow in professional competence they must learn to be more aware of place phenomena than the average person.

Opportunities to Explore

The third dimension concerns the extent to which a job has a space-time structure that allows a worker freedom to seek out and explore new settings, either as a regular part of or an adjunct to the work. Some mail carriers are able to take advantage of this, as are home appliance repair people, delivery people, and the like. In fact, there was a bad example a few years ago that showed how great this opportunity can be. The English city of Cambridge was terrorized in 1975 by an unknown rapist who always eluded capture by quickly disappearing. Police theorized that he must be in a trade that had helped him to develop detailed knowledge of the city. When finally caught, he turned out to be a delivery driver for a local firm. His day-to-day job movements had afforded him many opportunities to learn the by-ways and back streets of Cambridge in better detail than most other people.

The writer John Bunyan provides a happier example of a person whose trade produced exploration experiences that he was able to turn to advantage in writing. As a traveling tinker, Bunyan had opportunities to observe the people and settings of his area and then incorporate them into his books. Even when they do not have another trade, writers have more freedom from specific space and time requirements (they generally do not have to go to the office each day). They therefore have more freedom to explore and to experiment with their settings, which often leads to a strong spirit of personal place.

Moving around town: the mailman.

The catch-all term of naturalists also fits here, as their work can include considerable wandering about and investigating new settings. In fact, this process is so central to understanding the natural world that these people could well have been included in the previous category of occupations where place awareness is central to the task. I feel that Gavin Maxwell's books about his life with otters (such as *Ring of Bright Water*) were as much about the spirit of place he created for himself and his animals, as they were about the animals themselves.

I discussed tramps earlier, and they should be mentioned again on this dimension. Their life of movement and few permanent ties provides the opportunity for many rich place experiences for those who can use it. A similar freedom in mobility exists for nomadic shepherds, gypsies, and other groups whose basic life and work structure calls for frequent changes of location.

Location and Experience Patterns

Nomads also illustrate the situation in which people have experiences as a result of spending considerable amounts of time in certain locations. Another example is construction of facilities such as roads, bridges, extraction plants, power generating stations, and the like, in remote areas. Such workers particularly remember the heightened sense of their surroundings that prevailed while they were on the assignment. The building of the Alaska pipeline and construction of the North Sea oil rigs are the two most publicized recent examples. (The disastrous collapse of one of the North Sea platforms in early 1980 also highlights the risks that often accompany extreme place experiences.)

The construction site can become a self-contained, but everchanging world for its workers.

Farmers and country veterinarians would both tend to develop place sensitivity from their work location, for reasons already discussed. (I did not include farmers in the "freedom to explore" dimension, because their lives usually have relatively little of that, being tied to their farms by the demands of work that often cannot be put off.) English veterinarian James Herriot described the joys and insights that come from the country setting of the veterinarian, even while being swamped with work:

> And having [the new dog] with me added so much to the intermissions I granted myself on my daily rounds. Whereas in offices and factories they had tea breaks I just stopped the car and stepped out into the splendour which was always at hand and walked for a spell down hidden lanes, through woods, or as today, along one of the grassy tracks which ran over the high tops.
>
> (James Herriott, *All Things Bright and Beautiful*)

The emphasis here has been on an occupation's strength as a stimulator of place awareness. It is perhaps obvious that we could also make qualitative distinctions between occupations that generate equally strong but different senses of place in their members. For instance, in a study of definitions of "neighborhoods" in Springfield, Massachusetts, it was found that taxi drivers, urban planners, and public health nurses each had well-developed but quite different views of neighborhood boundaries, with each based on the informational needs of their own particular professions.[5]

I have not dealt with the large number of non–place occupations that do not stimulate much awareness of settings. Such jobs as assembly-line work, clerical posts, white-collar office jobs, and shop-keeping have little or none of these dimensions. This is not to say that low awareness is always the result of these kinds of jobs, but rather that the ways they are organized and structured have a dulling rather than a sharpening effect on people's awareness of their surroundings. One of the purposes of increased efforts at improving the quality of work life in large organizations is to provide a more interesting sense of place.

The railyard: a setting that's home to a railroader no matter where in the country it's located.

There is also an implication that we could learn about the experience of place from people in certain occupations. For instance, if we want to know more about how settings are used, we could ask real estate agents (for permanent settings such as homes) and park rangers (for temporary settings such as camp sites.) There is a store of knowledge here that other people have not used to much advantage.

I hope that this chapter's ideas can be of similar use to readers. If we understand the impact of different occupations better, we should be better able to choose our own jobs based on matching our desires to the total experience pattern (location, exploration, and so on) they provide, not just to the content of the work itself. Personnel selection procedures could also be improved by identifying place people (as in Chapter 5) who value the process of learning about settings for its own sake.

Many jobs could be redesigned to take more advantage of potential place experiences, thus providing another reward to the worker. There will always be occupational roles (naturalist, archaeologist, landscape artist) that have inherent advantages in providing place experiences, but the potential place value of many jobs goes unrealized. It could be increased, for instance, by using the task demand dimension, and allowing workers to have more influence over their immediate work settings. Flexible working hours can also provide people a chance to see surrounding areas that they have never had a chance to explore in the rigid 8-to-5 format.

Do we know whether certain occupations create place awareness, or whether people who are aware of place choose certain occupations? I would still say that it depends, and that the influence works both ways. That is, a person who works as a forest ranger is likely to become more sensitive to natural settings, no matter how he or she starts out, while forestry is also more likely to attract people who are interested in natural settings and their proper maintenance and renewal. Both are reasonable influences, and the only thing that I think should be reemphasized is that it is just as legitimate to seek out a job because of where it is done as for its content. If you are in an occupation that has stimulated your awareness of the sense of place, there may be ways to apply it in a new area when you tire of the original occupation.

NOTES

1. Harold Nicolson, *Diaries and Letters*, Vol. 3 (Nigel Nicolson, ed.), London: William Collins Sons, Ltd., 1968, pp. 223–224.

2. Edwin Way Teale, *A Naturalist Buys an Old Farm*, New York: Dodd Mead & Co., 1974, p. 127.

3. Roger Warner, "Riding Freights is no Picnic for Tramps Today," *Smithsonian*, Vol. 6, No. 9, 1975, p. 95.

4. Ronald Blythe, *Akenfield: Portrait of an English Village*, New York: Delta, 1970, pp. 191–200.

5. Barry Greenbie, "Contrasting and Consistent Perceptions of Neighborhood Boundaries in a New England City," *Man-Environment Systems*, Vol. 5, 1975, pp. 325–327.

12 Variety or Depth? The Micro-World Experience

We now turn to consideration of a different kind of long-term place effect, one that is the result of where we choose to live and work. The most extreme versions of this pattern are to move frequently and experience a variety of settings, or to locate in one or a few spots in a lifetime and experience a sense of place in depth. For most of us, this poses a dilemma: if we choose variety we have given up the depth experience, and if we opt to stay in one spot we have lost the experience of variety and change.

I would guess that most readers today are relatively familiar with the pattern of movement and some variety in locations. Others may have spent a good portion of their time in one place. This short chapter focuses on two aspects of these choices: the micro-world experience, or getting to know a limited setting in great depth; and the process for developing a strategy for finding depth and variety in one's place experiences.

THE MICRO-WORLD EXPERIENCE

Very simply, "micro-world experience" means coming to know a limited setting in great depth, and focusing on increasingly fine details and new relationships among them. This goes beyond "learning the ropes," and includes both knowing a setting in many intimate ways and coming to know oneself better in relation to that setting.

For example, the groundskeeper who has worked for ten years or so at one major league baseball park has the opportunity to really know that park as a micro-world: he has seen it full of people and empty, in good weather and bad, in and out of the baseball season, in good shape and needing attention. He knows walkways, locations of equipment, decorative elements, patterns of wind and light, and so on. Most of these details are invisible to the average short-term visitor to the park, but they are part of the fabric of the groundskeeper's world, and are often loved as such.

To take a more exotic example, consider the experience of art connoisseur Bernard Berenson in his adopted home near his Italian villa:

> For the afternoon walk we drove up the hills behind Vincigliata, often for several miles, and then walked down to find the car at an appointed place. Mr. Berenson had spent thirty years exploring these hills and he knew every path. Each walk had its own name, often that of some friend who had discovered it. . . . Every hundred yards he would stop in ecstasy, sometimes at a distant view, more often at a group of farm houses, or the roots of an old olive tree, or at a cluster of autumnal leaves and seed pods. He would be completely absorbed in what he saw, speechless with delight. His conversation on these walks was often about the strange characters who had lived in the villas and farms, or about old friends.
>
> (Kenneth Clark, *Another Part of the Wood*)

A baseball groundskeeper and an expatriate art connoisseur may have different lives, but they suggest that one can have a micro-world experience because one works regularly in one spot, or because one relaxes regularly there, and both situations can provide a strong sense of identity and enjoyment.

Features of the Experience

When we look at it analytically, this experience has several key features, which taken together, distinguish it from other experiences related to sense of place.

Time Spent Regularly in the Setting   Although this alone is not sufficient to provide a real micro-world experience, it is necessary; one has to be in a place enough to allow depth experiences to happen. Berenson had over thirty years' history with the hills behind his villa.

Taking the time to just be around: bench life on the Boston Common.

Seeing More and More   People who have micro-world experiences discover new elements in settings they thought they knew completely. This discovery can occur gradually, as when someone keeps noticing new details in buildings along the street, and looking still closer, seeing things such as how the roofs are made and how the entrances vary. The discovery process also occurs as specific breakthroughs, such as being in a familiar meadow and deciding on a whim to get down on the ground and see what's there, thus opening up a new world of plants, rocks, soil, and insects that was unnoticed underfoot before.

Seeing Patterns   Over time, we can not only discover new elements, but also patterns of how they relate to one another. A long-term resident of a city neighborhood learns how transport systems tie one neighborhood to others, how services vary in different parts of the neighborhood, where water collects after rains, how well or badly the various social subgroups get along with each other, which locations are likely to breed one failed business after another, and many other patterns.

Seeing Changes in Patterns   A higher level of micro-world experience is to become aware of changes in patterns and relationships among elements. This definitely requires the person's presence continuously. Doris Lessing described just such a period in her short story, "A Year in Regent's Park," in which a woman's experiences with the micro-world of London's Regent's Park through a full year are described, and changing patterns of vegetation, weather, and human activities are seen to influence each other through the seasons.[1]

Special Meanings   As the Berenson example makes clear, different elements in the setting take on particular meanings, usually because of previous events or feelings that become associated with that element. The setting grows richer with successive layers of memories, so that it evokes many more feelings and associations than could an objectively "richer" setting with which one has only a short history. These layers of meaning are one of the reasons people often find it hard to leave a setting that has become their micro-world.

Better and Worse Material   Of course, some settings are rich, others are relatively barren. On the average, rural settings have a high potential for diversity and variety, or what is sometimes called "fine-grained diversity." (Residents who long for somewhere else may not see this, however.) Large, complex cities can also serve well as micro-worlds, as they contain so many elements and patterns to be discovered. It is often this experience that makes residents love cities that seem unlivable to outsiders.

Almost any setting has enough features and patterns in it to become a micro-world for someone who can be open to seeing what is there and valuing experiences. There are some, however, that for the average person are less likely to stimulate that experience. For instance, there is a certain style of large, homogeneous American suburban housing development that looks the same wherever it is located, contains relatively few variations in detail (especially in early years before shrubs and trees have grown enough to differentiate homes from each other), and has lost whatever original natural features there were through the process of building and filling in all the available space.

Another type of poor micro-world setting is the isolated place in which people are more or less forced to remain, such as prisons or the more remote military outposts. A U.S. Navy officer once described to me the effects of the

A well-sited farm can be an engrossing micro-world.

THE LONG-TERM IMPACT OF SPIRIT OF PLACE

"rock fever" suffered by Navy personnel when they had been stationed too long on an island off the coast of Alaska: they yearned to leave, paid no attention to their setting, and became less able to use the potential resources that were there, all of which tended to block out their micro-world experiences.

There are settings that are poor micro-worlds unless a person can make a major investment in discovering their hidden potential. These have more subtle features, and require time and energy in order for one to see anything new there. For example, the Great Plains area of the United States is felt by many easterners to have "nothing in it," and to represent a blank space to be ignored when driving across the country. They would see Cape Cod, on the other hand, as a rich setting with much to see, do, and explore. Having grown up in Kansas, I feel that the Great Plains are just as rich as Cape Cod, but with much more subtle colors, land forms, and wild life patterns. They therefore require more of an investment of time and attention in order for what is there to be seen.

THE PERSON'S PART IN THE MICRO-WORLD EXPERIENCE

The example of needing to tune in to the plains setting in order to see what is hidden but available, is consistent with our view that sense of place is created by both the setting and the person. There are certain personal factors that help determine whether an individual will be likely to have strong micro-world experiences.

Attitude

An obvious factor is the attitude one has concerning what rewards will come from within the limited bounds of the setting: most helpful is positive expectation that there are worthwhile items to be seen, experiences to be had, things to be learned. As Gaston Bachelard described it, "People never tire of recalling that Leonardo da Vinci advised painters who lacked inspiration when faced with nature to contemplate with a reflective eye the crack in an old wall. For there is a map of the universe in the lines that time draws on these old walls."[1]

Perceptual Skills

A related factor is the ability to perceive, imagine, focus, and so on, so that the richness of the setting becomes clear. Not everyone is a Leonardo, able to see the world in a cracked wall; but most of us have more potential for observation, imagination, and new perceptions than we generally use. Taking a small spot, such as a patch of ground or the corner of a room, and trying to see everything that is there, is a good self-training device. More details emerge with practice, even when repeating the exercise in a spot whose possibilities seemingly had been completely described.

Feelings about the Process

These skills are more likely to produce a rich micro-world experience if one also likes being open to the richness of limited settings. Naturalist Henry Beston once wrote:

> Who would live happily in the country must be wisely prepared to take great pleasure in little things. Country living is a pageant of nature and the years; it can no more stay fixed than a movement in music, and as the seasons pass, they enrich life far more with little things than with great, with remembered moments rather than the slower hours.
>
> (Henry Beston, *Northern Farm*)

Beston also described how people do well in the country if they seek small pleasures, such as colors reflected from snow, or the changes in the smells of a farm house through the year.

Feelings about Being in a Particular Setting

The pleasures you get from a setting are in turn influenced by another factor: how you feel about being there at all. If you are living in a place by choice, it is a more free experience than if you are coerced to remain there, as in the example of prisons or military posts. If you are coerced, considerable energy, anxiety, and attention can be drained off into either anger about the situation or plotting possible means of escape, and you are unlikely to be open to any features except escape hatches. This pattern is partly responsible for farm youths rejecting the country pleasures of their childhood as they look yearningly toward the excitement (and expected freedom) of the city. Their micro-world has little value to them, and feels more like a prison than a rich set of opportunities, whereas someone who chooses to move to a farm sees a grand network of new features and experiences opening up. It can be the same farm for each, but it is certainly a different sense of place.

Loose Time Structures

Finally, a major factor is the time and activity structure that governs a person's uses of energy and attention. In order to be attuned to a setting regularly and explore it in detail, one has to schedule activities there to avoid the need always to be hurrying to go somewhere or do something else (see photo on p. 115). It is much harder for hurried people to have a micro-world experience, as they have programmed themselves not to be able to follow up unexpected events or new possibilities. This is one reason many white-collar workers feel alienated from their surroundings. Their days are so programmed as to where they will be, what they will do, and when, that there are no spontaneous experiences, no surprises, and therefore no real contacts with the details of their settings.

Who, then, are the most likely people to have rich micro-world experiences? Who would tend to have positive attitudes and expectations, perceptual skills, receptive feelings about being in a setting, and a loose time-space structure so that there is a chance for new perceptions? A few examples include naturalists, farmers, children, elderly people, and residential university students.

Naturalists   As already noted, naturalists tend to have a general curiosity about how the world works, plus a professional interest in learning about certain areas. Edwin Way Teale has achieved real growth with his study of the insect world in his back garden; and there is, of course, Gilbert White's eighteenth century English classic, the *Natural History of Selborne*, recording his experiences in naturalist observation through letters to friends describing his immediate neighborhood. He did not try to travel to the far corners of the globe in order to understand natural life, but rather chose to try to know one setting extremely well. The natural sciences may have surpassed some of his early content, but they have never surpassed his ability to evoke a sense of place; thousands of enthusiasts visit Selborne every year to try to capture some of White's micro-world experience. They would, in fact, do better at this if they were to concentrate on getting to know their own settings, a process that would be more in White's spirit.

Farmers   People who work the same land over long periods probably know their setting better than anyone else. This is partly out of necessity: their livelihood depends on understanding the land and its relationships to plant and animal inhabitants, so that the supportive potential of the farm can be realized without destroying it in the process. I believe that most farmers also develop other reasons for their awareness that relate to the sheer joy of knowing a setting as well as (or better than) they know themselves. The influence probably works both ways: a person gets to know the setting well in order to farm, and farms in order to get to know the setting well.

Children and Older People   They are most likely to need to use their immediate settings intensively, and therefore are most in need of rich settings full of diversity. This need has two basic causes: (1) these people are less mobile and more dependent on others, so that their range of physical setting experiences is naturally constricted; and (2) they have looser time-activity structures that allow more slack for exploration and enjoying settings for their own sake. In other words, unless the family pattern is one of frequent geographic movement (to new jobs, or for whatever other reasons), both youngsters and old people are likely to have the experience of getting to know their settings in great detail. In addition, the nature of children's time focuses them on more of the details, and they experience their relationship to a setting as having lasted longer:

> In relating the passage of time to the experience of place it is obviously necessary to take the human life cycle into account: ten years in childhood are not the same as ten years in youth or manhood. The child knows the world more sensuously

Children invest great psychological energy in knowing and using the parts of their circumscribed world.

than does the adult. This is one reason why the adult cannot go home again. This is also one reason why a native citizen knows his country in a way that cannot be duplicated by a naturalized citizen who has grown up elsewhere.

(Yi-Fu Tuan, *Space and Place*)

In other words, a child may spend two years in a setting and experience more of the micro-world point of view than an adult spending five years in the same (or any other) place.

University Students   I am thinking here primarily of residential students, who live for a period of time within the bounds of a compact university community. The effects of this are to reduce mobility and the conflicting demands on them to be elsewhere, and to compress activities into a fairly dense, limited area, so that travel time and other peripheral energy drains are reduced. When people recall their "good old college days," I believe that they feel this attachment precisely because it was a micro-world experience. They were able to focus on one setting in depth, with enough slack time and other people who had similar interests so that they could share rich, spontaneous experiences in a concentrated time period.

Part-time and commuter college programs often do not generate such a loyal emotional attachment. This difference is sometimes laid to status or social class differences (such as people not wanting to identify with a truncated educational experience), but I think it is more likely to be caused by a space-time structure that does not provide a micro-world experience: the students are spread too thin among home, school, and work settings, with not enough time and opportunity in any of them.

THE LONG-TERM IMPACT OF SPIRIT OF PLACE

A micro-world that people remember for a lifetime: the university.

(Courtesy of the British Tourist Authority)

Personality Types In addition to these likely categories, there are probably certain personality dimensions that could allow us to predict who would enjoy and respond well to micro-worlds. This could be the subject of a study in its own right, but I just suggest here that one useful characteristic would be the tendency to approach situations as a *perceiver*, to see what is there; as opposed to a *judger*, whose attitude is one of deciding whether what is there is right or wrong, good or bad. Being open allows one to relax enough to see new things, as opposed to staring at the setting with an evaluating eye.[3]

CHOOSING LOCATIONAL STRATEGIES

Even with these examples of people who will have richer micro-world experiences, we all still have the option to choose our locations and activities so as to increase or decrease depth and variety in our sense of place. Why would we choose to seek to understand a micro-world in depth? One reason, as has been mentioned, is survival. Another is to gain a territorial advantage. A whole book could be written on the impact of the micro-world on human social relationships. One of the fundamental consequences of staying in one spot for a long period is that one shares a continuous history with others. This network of shared history, memories, and events is what people often think of when they are asked what the term "neighborhood" means to them.

The bounded, yet ever-changing world of a small river.

Many of the examples in this chapter have implied the sheer pleasure and sense of joy that people can obtain from a good micro-world experience. It can clearly be an end in itself, adding zest to life. To take one case, I think that the avid trout fly-fisherman often gets as much pleasure from the micro-world experience as he does from the fishing process per se. Getting to know a good fishing river has a number of parts to the experience: locating particular pools; learning the behavior patterns of fish in these pools; noticing different scenes along the banks; knowing the river at different water levels; seeing changes in the river from year to year; and learning social norms for fishing the river and relating to other fisherman who use it regularly. In other words, repeated fishing experiences in one area of one river are not actually repeating the same experience; nor are they concerned simply with fish and gear. For keen fishermen, a whole micro-world draws them in and holds them fascinated, or keeps them coming back again and again to experience a valuable sense of place.

The micro-world experience also serves as a complement or contrast to more varied, larger-scale stimulation. Some people obtain this by periodically withdrawing to the same micro-world, as Sir Winston Churchill did to his country home, where he shaped his own world through gardening, building walls, and painting; or President John F. Kennedy to the family compound at Hyannisport, Massachusetts. For each there was a sense of renewal and regeneration in the setting's contrast with large-scale national and world affairs.

An alternate means of obtaining complement is to shift one's life pattern radically for different phases. Author P. G. Wodehouse and his wife shifted in late middle-age from a nomadic lifestyle to being rooted in their Remsenberg, Long Island, home. They felt as good about not traveling as they had felt about traveling, having accepted the notion that their needs had changed.[4] They did not, as some of us do, try to hang onto a past style of living out of a conviction that it suited the "kind of people" they were and would always be.

THE LONG-TERM IMPACT OF SPIRIT OF PLACE

The idea of complement also takes us back to where this chapter started: the tendency of depth and variety to be mutually exclusive options. One way out of this dilemma (if one in fact wants both experiences) is to work on the contrast principle: either withdrawing periodically to the same micro-world setting, like Churchill, so that one can know it in depth; or shifting patterns as needs change, like the Wodehouses, so that there is variety during one period and depth at another.

The need for a life strategy which allows at least some in-depth place experiences has become more acute as industrial societies have spawned what Alvin Toffler (in *Future Shock*) called "the new nomads": families that move so frequently for work-related reasons that they are always in transition, always settling in or preparing to move to the next job location. The problem for the new nomads is that they do not carry their physical surroundings (tents) or social context (tribe) with them as do actual nomads. Thus they have few place experiences of depth, just that of the moving process itself. This is a psychologically costly pattern, and more and more families are beginning to question it, even to the point of deciding to turn down otherwise desirable promotions if they require still another geographic move.

As I have tried to make clear in this chapter, deciding to stay in one place for a while is not enough to produce a good micro-world experience, but it is at least a start. In addition, family members need to do some design work in terms of their time and activity scheduling, the relationship between home and work settings (e.g., not so far apart as the usual case today), and their own expectations about their setting and how it can be used. Whether they choose depth or variety, the most important point is to have some strategy around locational choices, so that they do not end up with some sort of bland, in-between non-experience.

NOTES

1. Doris Lessing, *The Temptation of Jack Orkney and Other Stories*, New York: Alfred A. Knopf, 1972.

2. Gaston Bachelard, *The Poetics of Space*, Boston: Beacon Press, 1968, p. 144.

3. The perception-judgment dimension of personality was originally formulated by C. G. Jung.

4. See David Jasen, *P. G. Wodehouse: A Portrait of a Master* (New York: Mason and Lipscomb, 1974, pp. 231, 246).

5. For interesting research on the impact of isolated settings, see Irwin Altman and William Haythorn, "The Ecology of Isolated Groups" (*Behavioral Science*, Vol. 12, 1967, pp. 169–182).

PART FIVE

THE SHORT-TERM EFFECTS OF THE SENSE OF PLACE

13 Rich Responses: Memories and Fantasies

Having considered some of the general long-term effects of settings' spirit of place, the four chapters in this part of the book are concerned with the more immediate short-term effect on users, whether residents or visitors. The emphasis is on understanding the potential of settings to spark interesting responses, and the ways in which these responses are the products of the mix of personal characteristics and features of the setting.

Assuming that our immediate responses are partly the result of what we bring to it, it is not necessary to be in an elaborately designed setting in order to have a good place experience. We supply a great deal of the richness by our responses, especially the two kinds I want to discuss in this chapter: the memories and fantasies that are set off by being in a particular setting. Although the two are not completely separate, for simplicity's sake I will discuss some of the basic qualities of each separately.

MEMORIES AND SETTINGS

The term "memories" refers to a whole class of images, thoughts, and feelings, which, when we experience them, have the quality of coming back to

125

us from the past. We sense that their source is within us, that we are suddenly connected to previous times and settings; and that our minds contain images that have been stored and are now retrieved.

To some extent we are always having memory experiences, as we generally react to any situation with previously learned responses (e.g., I do not have to relearn how to use a pencil each time I want to write a line for this book). The memories we are concerned with here are not the large store of regular, programmed responses, but rather the special, powerful, fleeting images that are not recurring, and that contribute to a special sense of place in particular settings.

Cues That Set Off Memories

Chapter 3 sketched briefly some ways in which sensory information combines with our basic perceptual processes to create images for us. This same information sets off our place memories, and they are usually stimulated by several types of cues.

Smells   Our sense of smell appears to be the most powerful trigger for unconscious memories: they can be recalled more quickly and powerfully by smells, with less thought and organization in the mind, than by any other signals. As author-hiker Colin Fletcher described this process so aptly:

> I am always being reastonished at the way our sense of smell can bring memories flooding back. Several months after I came up out of the (Grand) Canyon—when I was deeply embroiled once more in the complexities of the man-made world—I was checking over some old equipment when I chanced on the blue nylon poncho-groundsheet that I had spread out for the first time that evening in Hualpai Canyon. It was by now anything but brand-new. I lifted it up and saw that it was still tinted red with Grand Canyon dust. And at once I smelled the dust. I can find no adequate way to describe what my nose reported, for when it comes to smells our language is poverty-striken. But I know that the instant I smelled the dust from that tattered poncho there surged back into my mind the reality of what life in the Canyon had been like. I do not mean just that I remembered specific details. I knew once more in a flood tide of certainty that invaded all my senses, the forgotten essence—the whole clean open, sunlit, primitive freedom of it.
>
> (Colin Fletcher, *The Man Who Walked Through Time*)

Each of us probably has our own library of smells that serves as a time machine for transporting us instantly to associated settings. For myself, the smell of fresh Brussels sprouts never fails to return me into the Covent Garden market area of London where I had lived for a happy period.

This power may be because of the nonverbal, nonrational basis of smell as a source of information, to some vestige of our distant animal heritage, or to the fact that smells can be so distinctive that they serve as relatively tight, pin-point–accurate signals to recall specific moods and memories (see also photo on p. 27). For whatever reasons, the fact is that smells are potent keys to unlocking our storehouse of memories. This is one reason why settings such as old houses are often evocative: they have acquired many distinctive smells with age and repeated use.

We would do well to preserve and value these characteristics. Unfortunately, the trend in the United States is to try to cover up "unseemly" odors and mask the richness of the setting's history under some bland or over-sweet fake atmosphere, or to eliminate smells altogether and create a dead spot as far as one's nose is concerned. The more we try to eliminate smells, the flatter we make the setting as a stimulus to memories.

Sounds Although sometimes less potent than smells, sounds also have the capacity to send images from the past flooding back. Each of us has personal key sounds that tie us to other times and other places: the hum of bees, the starting of an automobile engine, the wail of a siren, the whir of an electric razor, the crow of a rooster in early morning, the drone of a propeller-driven airplane on a summer afternoon. Any sound that was regularly present during periods of our lives can unlock memories. The sound of farm animals in early morning is a particularly potent jog to memory for those who have grown up in rural settings, as are the late night sounds of the city dying down (occasional honks, shouts, and sirens) for city dwellers.

The type of sound that is probably universal as a memory-jogger is, of course, music: and settings that have music as a regular feature are rich in connections between present and past. Hundreds of cinema film scenes have shown someone thrown into a reverie by the song on the jukebox in a small cafe, and it often takes just a few notes of a popular or classical theme to generate a wave of nostalgic images.

Visual Cues Sights are obviously also important in stimulating memories, as so much of settings' features are perceived by seeing. Sight seems to be less directly tied to memories than smell or hearing, because we always see selectively and develop regular patterns that control what we do and do not see. Because there is so much visual information in our surroundings, it is probably just as well (in avoiding overloads) that visual cues are somewhat slower to call up our memories.

Settings that have a strong identity and prominent features, call back more memories of previous experiences in them than do those with few recognizable features, a fact that seems to have been overlooked in the majority of development projects in the United States over the past thirty years or so. The effectiveness of identifiable features is one reason why historic sites with strong traces of the past are often so evocative; they contain images that are too strong simply to be absorbed under catch-all perceptual categories as "houses," "walls," or "roads." Turn of the century Main Street brick buildings in many Midwestern cities have this insistent quality for me, and are able to evoke memories of many other old areas that look quite different on the surface.

Simple details like paving stones, if noticed, can start us fantasizing about how they came to be there in that form.

Stan Denniston, a Toronto photographer, has developed a type of photographic work he calls a "reminder": two photographs are mounted side by side, one of a spot that reminded him of somewhere else he had been, and the second of that "somewhere else" to which he returned and photographed after being reminded of it. This is a perfect example of the power of a setting's visual cues.[1]

Color and texture are two other general qualities that can stir memories of other places. As I sat one morning looking at a small hill of grass and bare rock in New York's Central Park, I was suddenly transported to the northern highlands of Scotland, to the plains of western Kansas, and to a favorite area in the high back country of the Colorado Rockies, all in about a minute's time. When I reflected on the oddity of these memories stimulated in one of the world's busiest cities, they were clearly not odd at all: in each of the places I was remembering, I had had a moment of seeing colors and textures (of both grass and rocks) very much like the hillside I now faced.

Finally, memories of earlier events in a particular setting are often enhanced by traces of one's own impact on that setting—some visual reminders of the moment or event that created that difference or alteration. As Kevin Lynch has suggested:

> Personal connection is most effectively made by personal imprints on the environment. New customs might connect environments symbolically to personal experience. The stages of physical growth can be imprinted on our surroundings by height marks, foot or hand prints. Portraits and photographs may be mounted to give the place a visible genealogy.
>
> There can be temporary memorials for recent events, to be replaced later by permanent markings, if the event remains memorable.

(Kevin Lynch, *What Time Is This Place?*)

Old graveyards have a spirit which seems to stir memories and thoughts about the past, as well as about other experiences in similar spots.

We can generate a richer sense of place for ourselves in our day-to-day settings if we alter them visibly. At the very least, these alterations will bring back to us the processes we went through to create them and how we felt as we did it; and they often generate memories of other similar settings as well.

The Role of Memories in the Sense of Place

The last example implicitly suggests two broad classes of memories related to cues in settings. One concerns memories of events or feelings that occurred previously in that same setting. For these, the traces of personal markings become catalysts when mixed with images when we return to the site of some previous event in our lives. Such was the case when William Saroyan returned to a northern California railway station and experienced the same happy feelings he had felt there fifty years earlier:

> One year on my way home after work at the Postal Telegraph Office, around half past twelve at night, I remember arriving at the Santa Fe Depot just as a very long passenger train from San Francisco stopped and passengers began to get off.
>
> About two dozen members of a family were standing on the siding waiting for somebody. They were the Arkelians—Kirkor, his wife, his sons, his daughters, and other members of the family.
>
> All of the Arkelians laughed, roly-poly Eddie laughed, and I laughed. . . .
>
> Four months ago I went to the Santa Fe Depot in Fresno at eleven at night to catch the train to Chicago and New York, and I remembered exactly where Eddie had got off and where his family had stood, waiting for him. It made me laugh with happiness all over again.
>
> (William Saroyan, *Places Where I've Done Time*)

One of the side benefits of the increasing incidence of planned home births in the United States is the fact that the home setting will then be rich in cues that recall the struggle and exhilaration of that important family event. In the usual hospital birth, those setting cues remain in a room that mother, father, and child are likely to never see again.

Settings in which unhappy events occurred have the same (and perhaps more) potency for recalling moods and feelings: an employee relives the embarrassment of a bad performance when returning to the boss' office; a person who has fallen ill in a restaurant feels the queasiness on returning to eat there; and almost anyone begins to sweat when approaching the site of earlier indignities in the dentist's office.

Novelist John Cheever has described Boston's ability to set off a negative sense of place because of his memories:

> I was in Boston when I was 17 and I thought I had gotten away completely. When I returned I found I had made no progress at all. All the images, all the ghosts and anxieties I thought I had escaped were still there. I couldn't, for example, go to Symphony Hall because my mother was there. There were whole areas of the city I couldn't go into. I was not mature enough to return to the scene of the crime.
>
> (Susan Cheever Cowley, "A Duet of Cheevers," *Newsweek*, March 14, 1977)

As we saw in Chapter 12, a micro-world setting that someone knows in depth will usually have a wealth of cues that bring back memories.

Memories can be triggered by qualities of a setting that recall moments in other settings. Many of the examples used earlier were of this kind, where one's sense of some element or pattern brought back a flood of images and feelings. Thus recollections occurred even though one had never experienced these actual elements before. These are memories through, but not of, the setting.

Old American houses hold the ability to take us back to earlier periods, if their sites are also preserved.

One instance of this is the memory triggered by an historic setting that has many well-known associations with the past. We obviously do not really remember events there—we have fantasies or imagine what life would have been like in them. We may remember hearing or reading about them; we may remember our previous visits there or to similar sites; but we do not actually have memories of life there. Our current visit to the setting is also generating associations that become the material for future memories.

Sometimes our memories of past settings are so strong that they haunt us, and we search for some way to return. In fact, memories have generally elaborated, simplified, and reshaped the original settings so that they exist only in our minds and not in reality.

> Stourwater was certainly dramatic yet how unhaunted, how much less ghost-ridden than Stonehurst; though perhaps Sir Magnus himself might leave a spectre behind him. In my memory, the place had been larger, more forbidding, not so elaborately restored. In fact, I was far less impressed than formerly, even experiencing a certain feeling of disappointment. Memory, imagination, time, all building up on that brief visit, had left a magician's castle (brought into being by some loftier Dr. Trelawney), weird and prodigious, peopled by beings impossible to relate to everyday life. Now Stourwater seemed nearer to being an architectural abortion, a piece of monumental vulgarity, a house where something had gone very seriously wrong.
>
> (Anthony Powell, *The Kindly Ones*)

This fictional example suggests that some of our enjoyable place experiences may be better recaptured in another setting with certain similar features than they are in the original. It is hard to duplicate a sense of place that no longer exists, as we, the social context, and usually the physical setting itself, have changed. The place we remember now exists only inside our head.

Several points are suggested by this. One is that our currently experienced settings can be enhanced by cues that trigger memories and associations of past feelings, thoughts, and images. The addition of past memories increases the complexity and enjoyment of presently perceived settings. Whether in country or city, our memories expand the world beyond a single point, allowing us to experience images and feelings in new and varied combinations.

Another implication is that we can engage in repeated use of a particular location and not have duplicate place experiences. For example, when exploring a new area for hiking, I try to use a particular section of trail at least twice, because the second experience is very different than the first, even though a casual observer might say that I had "repeated" my walk. The second is different because my memories of the first walk reduce surprise and uncertainty, but also add the qualities of recognition and anticipation that were absent when the details of the path were totally unknown. It is also different because I now have some sense of where the path ends, I know that it is manageable and that survival is not an issue, and I am therefore more free to focus on details that I missed the first time through. The issue of repetition then comes down to the question, repetition of what? Repetition of geographic location does not automatically mean repetition of place experiences. It will be just that, however, if we block out our memories and associations and simply go through the motions again without bringing anything of ourselves to the setting.

THE ROLE OF FANTASY AS A PLACE
RESPONSE

I have become convinced that one of the most important types of short-term responses to settings is fantasy: the imaginings, daydreams, and scenarios that occur in our heads but use our immediate surroundings as the stimulus. In fact, I believe that any setting that tends to encourage fantasies will have a consistently strong spirit of place, and any person who is open to free fantasizing will have richer place experiences than someone who is not.

It must be clear that when I talk about a setting being the stimulus for fantasies, I am generally *not* referring to make-believe or mock-up settings such as the haunted house at Disneyland, settings that are pretend environments to simulate an experience. I am referring to the ability of natural, everyday settings to encourage fantasies and images in their users.

For example, consider John Hillaby's internal dialogue while hiking in Europe:

> I remember walking through the night for hours and hours, toward Herstal, where Charlemagne, that King David of the Dark Ages, held high court and put his seal to all manner of important decrees. Now Herstal, I knew very well, has become an industrial slum. In a letter Burgomaster Andrien had warned me that: 'Of that great period, alas, not a vestige now remains.' The foundations of the palace lie under the gas works. But as I trudged along that canal it pleased me to think of those who had walked that way nearly twelve centuries ago.
>
> I saw myself in the company of Paul the Deacon, Peter the Grammarian and Godescall the Illuminator. I wondered what I might say to that great scholar Clement the Irishman and Dungal and Durcuil. All holy men, all hastening towards Herstal at the king's command.
>
> (John Hillaby, *Journey Through Europe*)

In a similar manner, my interest in place fantasies was crystallized during evening walks through Covent Garden area when I realized that my great enjoyment of exploring both new and familiar settings comes partly from images of myself living in another period in history, or in this location in the present, past, or future, and so on. When in Covent Garden (especially when it was still a live market, but even now I do it), in my mind I practically became one of the workers. When I am doing a training program in an old country house that has been converted to a conference center, I do not think of myself as just temporarily there for my rather mundane purposes, but as living there permanently, as if it were P. G. Wodehouse's fictional gem, Blandings Castle, and I were its dotty peer.

A setting for fantasizing about a different style of life—the grand English Country house, Compton Wynyates.

(Courtesy of the British Tourist Authority)

Fantasies are enriching responses to settings, especially to those that are not parts of our regular lives. Gaston Bachelard has written an interesting exploration of the fantasy process (which he calls "dreaming of houses") in relation to the sense of place, in which he suggests:

> An excellent exercise for the function of inhabiting the dream house consists in taking a train trip. Such a voyage unreels a film of houses that one dreamed accepted and refused, without our ever having been tempted to stop, as we are when motoring. We are sunk deep in day-dreaming with all verification healthily forbidden. But lest this manner of travel be a gentle mania of mine, I should like to quote the following from Thoreau's Journals, of October 31, 1850.
>
> "I am wont to think that I could spend my days contentedly in any retired country house that I see; for I see it to advantage now and without encumbrance; I have not yet imported my humdrum thoughts, my prosaic habits, into it to mar the landscape."
>
> (Gaston Bachelard, *The Poetics of Space*)

In other words, one of the best features of fantasizing about place is the lack of responsibility it entails—the freedom to play with images, scenarios, and moods, and imagine life any way you wish without having permanently committed yourself to anything. This works equally well from a low-flying airplane, which provides a view of the structure of sites rather than just houses per se.

Each person has particular mixes of elements, themes, and cues that will begin particular fantasies. In addition, I suspect that many people also have what we might call basic fantasy scenarios: strong recurring fantasies that are stimulated by similar situations. One of my own was started by reading of the trip through the dark dense forest of Mirkwood in J. R. R. Tolkien's *Lord of the Rings* saga. When I am in a dark forest setting, I usually flip into being a member of the group making that perilous trip through Mirkwood, and each time is just as real as the last. Readers might ask themselves what their own basic fantasy scenarios are, or watch for them and where and when they occur.

A fairly common one might be called, "place envy": the feeling of wanting to be the people that you see when you are visiting a new setting. You wish you were they going about their daily routines, experiencing the various cycles and changes of the setting, and so on. You feel envy for them and their place, even though you may in fact live in one that is more interesting and better suited to your own style. You do not really want to be those people, full-time, but you do want to be able to try out the setting enough to get to know it and to know yourself in it.

Although I have yet to find anyone who has not experienced the place envy fantasy at least a few times, it is likely that the place people described in Chapter 5 are more likely to have these daydreams. For them, this is a basic scenario of imagination generated by their strong curiosity about new settings; for non–place people, it is an occasional fantasy stimulated by some particularly unusual or appealing setting.

Settings rich in identity and cultural symbolism are most often the subjects of fantasy. For example, the previously cited large old houses or mansions (see photos on p. 130 and p. 133) are storehouses of fantasies for those who would never be able to live in them, as people use them as vicarious spurs to daydreaming about other life styles. When local government authorities or developers systematically destroy these settings, they destroy something of people's capacity for collective imagination as well. Those homes have been a source for fantasies for both poor and rich: one does not have to own a setting for it to be a source of rich place experiences.

I do not mean to emphasize the upper class aspect of these houses as the only quality that triggers fantasies; fantasies can be about the humblest of places. If we spend most of our time in elegant settings, our fantasies can be sparked by a glimpse of a tenement or a junkyard; if we live in a sparse environment, we imagine life in the grand house that we see in passing. Fantasies in settings that are not our own add variety to our lives, and allow us to experience places in ways that are limited only by our imaginations. In this same regard, I think one of the overlooked functions of churches, cathedrals, and temples throughout history has been to be sources of fantasies for their users. The scale, complexity, and richness of decoration of a fine place of worship are acknowledged to be tributes to a divine presence; they also serve as settings with which people can identify, be a part of, and consider as their own, even though as individuals they could never own such a setting. The trend in the United States today toward simpler churches and functional necessities may make economic sense, but it also reduces the richness of people's experiences in them.

Common identity and fantasy: the church.

Another fantasy facility on a scale grander than individual means: the golf club.

The same is true for the trend toward simpler settings for college education. The older style residential campus provided a grander setting than many individuals could afford, with a history and many cues for fantasies, and all members of the college community could feel that they owned it. As was described in the micro-world discussion, attending classes in the evening in a converted city building is not as likely to breed fantasies or a strong sense of identification with place. In the other direction, it may be that the most grand new settings being built today as communal stimulators of place fantasy are the more elaborate indoor shopping malls, with their large spaces, changing levels, bright colors, and (usually) elaborate plantings (see photo on p. 13). A well-designed regional mall may play the same role (in terms of fantasy) that the medieval cathedral did in central Europe.

In addition to rich features, I believe that any locale will generate fantasies if we are inherently interested in the life, culture, and history of that area, and we are less likely to fantasize about those locations that do not interest us. For instance, I would probably generate more varied images and speculations on a walk through the Scottish countryside than by one through the Costa Rican countryside. This is nothing against Costa Rica and its settings; it is really a function of the interests that I bring with me.

A potent stimulus to fantasies of past eras, if you're interested: stone walls which once bounded New England fields now grown to woods.

THE SHORT-TERM EFFECTS OF THE SENSE OF PLACE

Loosening Up

Personal style and habits about place fantasies are developed mainly in childhood, that period of life in which our physical mobility is limited and we must therefore expand our range through imagination. In addition, the "business" of childhood includes playing, and playing can always legitimately include a large element of fantasy. As we grow older we learn new roles as adults, roles that are not supposed to include much daydreaming and fantasizing. From this chapter, it should be obvious that I think that this restriction is a costly one, and that if we follow this rule we block off some of our best opportunities for pleasure and stimulation. I believe that to get the most out of whatever settings we use, we should try to remain open to memories and fantasies, and pay attention to them as real experiences of place—just as real as temperature or the smell.

Memories and fantasies are central ingredients to rich place experiences, and we under-use our potential to enjoy our lives when we ignore them or spend too much time in low-stimulation settings. Those who create new built environments often seem bent on homogenization of settings and the purging of all elements that would stimulate users' memories and fantasies except for negative associations to other equally dull locations. Designers seem also to take little account of how to design for repeat experiences in settings, as if memory played no part in the sense of place. We will discuss later (Chapter 18) some ways of making places that enhance rather than filter out fantasies.

N O T E

1. See John Bentley Mays, "Denniston's Double-takes Illustrate Visual Memory" (*The Toronto Globe and Mail,* Tuesday, April 22, 1980, p. 12).

14 Patterns and Sequences: A Point Versus a Flow

Another way of understanding our short-term responses to place experiences is to examine some of the factors that produce similar senses of place for different people in a given setting. To do this I have selected two potent but often overlooked aspects: *patterns* and *sequences* of elements and experiences for a person through a period of time. Both create structures that provide consistent place responses.

THE NATURE AND IMPACT OF PATTERNS

When I use the term patterns, I simply mean consistent combinations of environmental elements experienced by a person such as things, structures, activities, or recurring events, the most consistent response to which is a result of the mixture rather than of any single element.

The idea I want to convey here is the difference between thinking of a place experience as an isolated point in our lives, and thinking of it as an element in a linked flow of events that have some structure and shape to their pattern. Two people may walk along the edge of the same farm field, at the same geographic location, but one of them lives 300 miles away, is there for the first time on a walking trip, and is going to visit a number of other areas as well; the other is the farmer who works that field, and has done so for the past 35 years, and has arrived there with a different purpose (to check drainage), and comes from 300 yards away rather than 300 miles.

The fact is that they are coincidentally at the same geographic point, but not at all at the same experiential point because the pattern of their lives is different; their sense of place is therefore likely to be different. The walker admires the scenery and is unaware that the farmer, who is so personally identified with the spot, feels past, present, and future beauty there that can only come from the pattern of his many experiences over time. The farmer, in turn, is unaware of the series of fields that the walker has passed through and the habits of care with land that have developed over many walking tours.

Another example of flow versus point involves achieving a sense of place that captures the true nature of an historic home. In the United States, the Plimoth Plantation in Massachusetts (site of the Pilgrims' early settlement in the 1620s) has recently allowed a group of students to live in the setting for five days, rather than simply visit it. The pattern of experience is quite different if one can experience changes over periods of the day or week, than if one is simply there for an hour. In this light, the notion of staying at an historic English country house such as Woburn Abbey as a "guest" of the Duke and Duchess of Bedford takes on a different meaning: it can provide a much deeper pattern of experiences relating to life in that type of setting, leading to a sense of place that is far different than stopping by for two hours on a day trip to see the area's sights.

Releasing Structures

Another important pattern occurs when a mix of elements serves as a releasing structure, allowing us to relax, loosen up, or release ourselves from certain constraints so that we are better able to have and enjoy place experiences in the present moment. Colin Fletcher provides a perfect example of such a pattern. When his camera was blown off its tripod and broken while he was hiking the Grand Canyon, he made a surprising discovery:

> I had brought only this one camera down into the canyon, and at first I simmered with frustration. But within an hour I discovered a new fact of life. I recognized, quite clearly, that photography is not really compatible with contemplation. Its details are too insistent. They are always buzzing around your mind and clouding the fine focus of appreciation. You rarely detect this interference at the time, and cannot do much about it even if you do. . . . But that morning of the Serpentine reconnaissance, after the camera had broken, I found myself freed from an impediment I had not known existed. I had escaped the tyranny of film. Now, when I came to something interesting, I no longer stopped, briefly to photograph and forget; I stood and stared, fixing truer images on the emulsion of memory.
>
> (Colin Fletcher, *The Man Who Walked Through Time*)

Many camera-toting tourists do not really experience a sense of place in the settings they visit. The photographic pattern focuses them on the future, imagining themselves showing their prints or slides, rather than on themselves in the settings in the present moment. This is not to say that taking pictures is necessarily bad, only that the responsibility to do it puts a different filter on one's sense of place.

A passage in the previous chapter described another releasing structure: being on a train and fantasizing about living in the houses you are passing. The structure of that situation is such that you have no chance to stop and explore any house in depth, so that making choices is not a responsibility; you are free to fantasize at will.

For people who travel frequently in their work, personal strategies for making travel arrangements can serve as a recurring releasing structure. For instance, allowing a comfortable cushion of time to get to the airport from my home has allowed me to see new things en route that I had never noticed before. It has become a travel experience in itself, whereas before it was dead space memorable only for my worrying about whether I was going to be in time for my flight. The cumulative effect of taking a little more time has been to save energy and provide me with a regular set of interesting new place experiences, a considerable gain for a small investment in a new pattern.

Time Patterns

This last example also implies another category of patterns: time-related structures. In many settings, our experiences are largely determined by time schedules: when facilities are open, how long we can use them (such as tennis courts), which services are available at given times, the hours established for work (and therefore of the flow of people to and from work), and so on. These structures mean that our experiences in a setting are shaped by when we are there (settings vary over time cycles, some faster and some slower) and whether we are in synchronization with the setting:

> The most common stress is synchronization, coordinating our time with another person's time, except in those joyful moments when we truly work together. Maurice O'Sullivan, writing of his boyhood off the Irish Coast, tells of his first trip to Dublin and of how the scheduling of the trains terrified him. Synchronization on his own island had been simple and coarse, signaled by the changes of daylight and made possible by patient waiting.
>
> (Kevin Lynch, *What Time Is This Place?*)

In other words, we are influenced in many ways, often unconsciously, by the patterns of time structures in our settings, both by what they allow us to do, and by the ease or difficulty we have in perceiving the patterns and synchronizing ourselves to them.

Another time-related structure is the pace or rate of travel, which has an obvious (but often overlooked) impact on how we see them. There are many settings, such as small dense urban neighborhoods, that require a walking pace in order for us to perceive them and get to know their details. Others, such as certain types of intimate countryside, benefit from a slightly faster rate of travel; roads in England's Cotswold Hills fall into this category:

> The right method of progression on the Whiteway is the bicycle. The swoops in the road are right, the bends are right, the changes in scene are right, the speed is right. Some roads are more detailed, and walking is better. Some more deadly dull and a car is right. But if you feel stuffed up and discontented, get on a bike up the Whiteway towards Calmsden and Chedworth.
>
> (Charles and Mary Hadfield, *The Cotswolds*)

The back roads of Vermont provide the same kind of experience at this moderate rate of travel, and this is no doubt the reason why a number of bicycle touring services have been established there in the last few years.

Moving through a landscape at a much greater speed in an automobile, a different kind of experience presents itself. We do not see the small details as they are blurred into an indistinguishable flow, but we do get a new kind of experience: a feel for the larger structure of the land, with its ups and downs and natural shifts. We become better able to feel the rhythm of the land and its relationship to the road. Certain areas, such as Kansas' Flint Hills region are particularly delightful when experienced this way. Thus rates of travel are not good or bad per se, but they do match up (in terms of a sense of place) with the setting through which you are traveling.

This house may have been preserved, but its patterns of use surely were not, once it was surrounded by roadways and parking lots.

THE SHORT-TERM EFFECTS OF THE SENSE OF PLACE

Pattern Through Repetition

Besides a particular combination of elements, many of these examples have another pattern quality, that of repetition or recurrence of specific experiences, so that one's sense of place is built up rather than obtained by any single instance. The cumulative effect of a number of responses on the person's sense of place is the main effect of this type of pattern.

One can consciously choose repetitive patterns of activities to increase new place experiences. For instance, the decision to spend some time each day just "hanging out" in a central spot in your town might seem just repetitious and the opposite of having new experiences. As a pattern, however, it has a cumulative effect: it increases the probability that you will see new aspects of the town you have not previously noticed, that you will have new experiences related to other people who spend time in the town center, and that you will see unusual events if and when they occur. The strategy is to allow yourself enough unstructured, non-purposeful time in a setting to allow perception of unpredictable parts. Once again, repetition of hours spent in the same physical location is not necessarily repetition of experiences; this depends on the richness of the setting and your ability to see new things in it. (See also Chapter 12 on the micro-world experience.) Unfortunately, many towns in the United States now have no active center. The shopping mall is the closest substitute, and in fact malls have become the new centers because they can fulfill this function.

THE IMPACT OF SEQUENCES

I would like also to examine the effects of a particularly interesting type of environmental experience pattern, namely, sequence. The order in which we experience different aspects of a setting influences how we see it and what we experience as a sense of place.

When tourists visit a country that is different from their own, they often do something, usually by accident, and late in their visit, such as paying a satisfying visit to an unknown and somewhat intimidating area, that eases their uncertainty of being in a strange place. If they had consciously sought some kind of unfreezing experience earlier (riding an unfamiliar transport system, going to an unknown area without a guide, trying to speak only the residents' language for a day, and so forth) they could have increased their range of place experiences over the full visit. In other words, an early challenging experience in a new setting is of more value than one occurring late in the trip. It changes expectations, thereby influencing how we see the setting, the kinds of choices we will make, and the amount of enjoyment we get from the new setting because we feel less anxious when using it.

Certain events early in a sequence can work against you. For example, when starting on a long hiking trip, it is important not to overstrain yourself in your beginning enthusiasm. If you do, you will be constantly fatigued and uncomfortable (and mainly focused on pain) throughout the rest of the trip; discomfort will be your most memorable experience.

Not an auspicious way to begin a stay in a hotel: passing under a wall of the hotel which is touting another place to stay.

Another common effect of sequences is their influence on how we feel about events. Our evaluations of a setting are often heavily influenced by how we got there and what our preceding experience was. A subordinate arriving at the boss' office for a meeting has often had to leave something he felt was important, make the effort to go somewhere, and pass through regions with symbols of authority (such as more elegant furnishings), all of which make him see the boss' setting differently than if he had been there all morning doing something else.

A more extreme example is the reaction of Major John Wesley Powell's nineteenth century exploring party emerging onto the plains area below the Grand Canyon, after the first (and extremely harrowing) trip through the Canyon by non-natives:

> No longer faced with the dangers and toils of rapids and white water, they drifted along on the calm river for another day. 'The relief from danger and the joy of success are great,' wrote Powell. 'How beautiful the sky, how bright the sunshine, what floods of delirious music pour from the throats of birds.'
>
> (Boyd Norton, *Rivers of the Rockies*)

In this case, a previous experience made a new setting feel better. It was indeed a different place, because the viewers arrived there through a special sequence of experiences.

THE SHORT-TERM EFFECTS OF THE SENSE OF PLACE

Sequence is an important variable in certain kinds of special-purpose settings, such as golf courses and museums. A nice case was Patrick Geddes' Outlook Tower in nineteenth century Edinburgh, a building with a display of interacting ecologic systems that was far ahead of its time:

> Geddes preferred visitors to start their journey through the Tower from the top. This could be reached by a winding back staircase, which by-passed all the rooms, and he liked to lead people up it at breakneck speed. When they emerged onto the narrow balcony around the Turret they would be gasping for breath, and he claimed that they experienced the sudden panoramic views more intensely when the blood was circulating rapidly through their bodies.
>
> (Paddy Kitchen, *A Most Unsettling Person*)

Even without the circulating blood, people would see the Tower's exhibits differently if they had started the exhibit by viewing the panorama of Edinburgh, a complex geosocio-ecologic system, spread out below them.

Sequence became an important variable in the design of great English country houses. Up until the eighteenth century, they had been built in a formal fashion, with rooms laid out serially. The deeper into the house the person was allowed to penetrate, the higher their status, as the rooms were symbolically related to power. Then in the eighteenth century the emphasis shifted to using the house for more active, structured social events with a mix of people, and therefore designs encouraged a "circuit" sequence for large assemblies, with a natural order to movement from room to room. The same change in emphasis occured in the lay-out of grounds: landscaping became the creation of a sequence of experiences for houseguests to enjoy as they made a circuit outdoors.[1]

Lobbies also set a tone in the sequence as does this striking one in the John Hancock Tower in Boston. Being there is a real event, not just on the way to somewhere else.

A modern example of sequence design is the Kaleidoscope, a children's activity center in the Crown Center shopping complex in Kansas City. The Kaleidoscope has several planned events as part of a session: the children pass through a series of spaces with visual and tactile exhibits to stimulate their awareness of themselves and other things; they then arrive in an activity center that contains a large variety of materials with which to experiment and make things; finally, they leave by passing through and stopping in a darkened space where slides and music reduce their feelings of excitement and bring them back down to earth. The children come out refreshed and stimulated, but not frantic, because the total place experience has a flow and sequence that leads naturally from one mood to another.

In the general case of museum design, inside flow may be well planned, while ignoring the larger sequence of events that determines how a person arrives at the museum in the first place (and therefore what mood they are in and how they use the museum). For instance, free admission directly shapes the experience of the museum as a place, as the question of whether to spend money is removed. This opens a range of uses from going all day to dropping in after work to look at only one interesting or favorite object. All of these uses are equally worthwhile, whereas having to pay for each visit raises the issue of getting value for money each time, and dampens spontaneity by making the quick trips seem too extravagant.

Finally, many of the sequences of place experiences in modern American life are so poor that we might almost suspect that they were intended to be that way: the long harrowing commute to a workplace we are supposed to enter smiling and energetic, when we feel mainly frazzled and competitive with the whole world; or the fine restaurant located in such an out-of-the-way place that we spend half the meal wondering whether we will ever find our way back home through the unfamiliar streets.

Patterns of experience are influenced by design choices: Boston visitors hunt for the subway entrances (such as the little black door here) without signs and begin to wonder if they are welcome at all.

THE SHORT-TERM EFFECTS OF THE SENSE OF PLACE

Patterns and sequences of place experiences can be unplanned or planned, accidental or consciously chosen. I believe we need to take a more active interest in them by asking such questions as: which events precede or follow each other best? Is there something I can do early in my use of a setting that will enrich later experiences there? Am I being influenced by a pattern structure that is relatively random? Which could I change by making different choices about where and when I do things?

Designers should ask similar questions: how will people get to this setting? Where will they be coming from, and in what kind of mood? How will they move through it? Where will they be expecting to go next?

Overall, it seems clear to me that we can design our own place responses more by paying closer attention to our choices and how they create patterns and sequences, both in the present and in planning future activities.

NOTE

1. Mark Girouard, *Life in the English Country House*, New Haven: Yale University Press, 1978, pp. 195, 210.

15 Instant Recognition: This Must Be the Place

One of the most familiar yet special short-term responses is the flash of instant recognition—the sense that one already knows a place that is being seen for the first time. We seldom come to a setting completely cold, but acquire images from various sources. In the first few moments there, we have a sense of place that is formed from both the actual setting and our built-up images through which we "know" it in advance and at a distance. For instance, here is a hiker's experience at the Arches National Monument in Utah's Canyonlands:

> I round the next bend in the canyon and all at once, quite unexpectedly, there it is, the bridge of stone.
>
> *Quite unexpectedly,* I write. Why? Certainly I had faith, I know the bridge would be here, against all odds. And I knew well enough what it would look like—we've all seen the pictures of it a hundred times. Nor am I disappointed in that vague way we often feel, coming at last upon a long-imagined spectacle. Rainbow bridge seems neither less nor greater than what I had forseen.
>
> (Edward Abbey, *Desert Solitaire*)

149

In other words, instant recognition is generated out of our preformed image, so that we may be physically in a place for the first time, but our perceptions make us feel that we have been there before. This is not to say, however, that the experience is always the same as what we expected. Consider Fletcher's first in-person view of the Grand Canyon:

> It was midmorning when we parked the car and walked across asphalt toward the Rim. I had seen my quota of photographs and paintings, of course, and thought I knew what to expect: an impressive view that no self-respecting tourist ought to miss.
>
> Long before we came close, I saw the space. A huge, cleaving space that the paintings and photographs had done nothing to prepare me for. An impossible, breath-taking gap in the face of the earth. And up from this void shone a soft, luminous light.
>
> . . . In that first moment of shock, with my mind already exploding old boundaries, I know that something had happened to the way I looked at things.
>
> (Colin Fletcher, *The Man Who Walked Through Time*)

Even with the preparation of advance images, we can be shocked by first experiences (although not necessarily with the impact it had on Fletcher, which was eventually to lead him to hike some 200 miles alone along the bottom of the Grand Canyon).

SOURCES OF IMAGES

There are many different sources of images for instant recognition: travel, newspapers, magazines, television and radio, books, travel posters, and promotional brochures. Travel writers (an endangered species) have played a major role in shaping these images. Among fiction writers, the authors of detective novels have contributed much, as the stories are often shaped by their settings, such as Rex Stout's Nero Wolfe novels set in New York, or John Creasey's stories of the Baron in London's Mayfair area. It is reported that an American couple visiting Oxford were relatively unimpressed with the university, but quite eager to see where various events had happened to Dorothy L. Sayers' fictional detective, Lord Peter Wimsey.

Stories that shape our expectations are not limited to the written word. Among non-print–oriented cultures such as the North American Eskimos, images are transmitted orally from generation to generation.

> This is the lake called Tulemaliguetna. The waters which lead to Tulemaliguak—the greatest of all inland waters—and the way to the ice sea in the north!
>
> We questioned him and it appeared that Ohoto had never seen this lake himself; nevertheless, he knew the subtle distinctions which told him its name, for such things are part of the common legend of travel that still lives on in the remaining tents of the Ihalmiut. Ohoto was right.
>
> (Farley Mowat, *People of the Deer*)

We all form childhood images of settings we have not yet seen: we hear family histories and other tales from parents and friends; we read stories set in particular locales; we read of historic events and generate visual images of their settings; we see settings on television and in movies; and so on.

For certain social and cultural groups of a society, the arts also form a major input to advance place images. James Morris' contact with French Impressionist paintings prepared him for a "return" to a setting he was visiting for the first time:

> I had to look up Trouville on the map but when I got there I knew it at once—not from any specific book or painting, but from a whole temper or genre of art. There lay the long empty foreshore, with only a few shrimp catchers knee-deep in its sand pools . . . and over it all, over the sands and the estuary and the distant promontory of Le Havre, there hung a soft impressionist light, summoned out of moist sunshine, high rolling clouds and the reflection of the sea. I knew the scene at once, from Monet and Bonnard and Proust.

> (James Morris, *Places*)

Certain magnets such as Trouville have drawn painters because of their special combination of light, natural features, and changing character. As noted in the discussion on certification, artists have often helped people to see new sides and new values in such settings, as well as publicizing them so that more people will experience them first hand.

HIGHLY VISIBLE SETTINGS

Although we receive information through many media, we obviously do not get equal amounts of information about all settings. Certain features help to determine whether many or few people will have formed images of a setting beforehand, and therefore experience instant recognition on the first visit. For instance, Peter Gould and Rodney White found that clear images of cities were directly related to the city's *population* (and therefore presumably to the activities and news it generated) and inversely to the *distance* of the perceiver from that city, as distance reduced the probability that they would hear or seek out news or other stories about the city.[1]

In similar studies of people's "mental maps," Lynch found that cities with distinct identity or spirit of place were more likely to be known, even by those who had not been there.[2]

Stanley Milgram makes a case for "international symbols," those locations that are famous all over the world, and which abound in Paris (the Eiffel Tower, the banks of the Seine, the Champs Elysées, and so on).[3] People are more likely to experience instant recognition on their first Paris visit because of these symbols, but what makes them international to begin with? I think a major contributor is the fact that Paris has been a long-standing prominent setting for world culture, with novels and stories in many languages having been set there. People all over the world thus come to feel that they "know" Paris without ever having been there, just as they do London, New York, and Rome for the same reasons.

Two examples of internationally-known features that are instantly recognized by first-time visitors: The Tower of London and a San Francisco cablecar.

THE SHORT-TERM EFFECTS OF THE SENSE OF PLACE

It is a circular process: locations become well known enough to draw people who provide their own reports, which helps others to form images:

> For reasons remaining foggy, I was favorably predisposed toward New York long before I saw it. In the chicken-tracked dirt yard of home, I constructed my version of "New York" from sticks of stove wood, random racks, tin cans, scrap lumber, whatever. . . .
>
> Books and movies are to blame, of course: I kept expecting back in 1946 to run into Nick Charles and Nora at some smart supper club where The Thin Man would gain no weight, no matter his intake of sophisticated calories; I anticipated becoming fast friends with Fiorello LaGuardia, and figured eventually to crony with Joe Dimaggio or to be discovered by a producer—while eating pickles at the Stage Delicatessen—who would force me to star in a Broadway play.
>
> (Larry L. King, *New Times*, April 30, 1976)

THE EFFECTS

There is no attempt to make a case for or against instant recognition, but it does exist as a response pattern and a contributor to our sense of place. It is, however, possible to make some general comments about its advantages and disadvantages. Whether this suggests that instant recognition is good or bad will depend on who you are, what you want, and the demands of a particular situation.

Even mundane items may be recognizable once seen in context, although taken for granted by residents: a London call-box.

One major advantage of preformed images is that they can help you to get more out of a place experience. For instance, during Fletcher's Grand Canyon hike he took a side trip to a long-abandoned (for over six hundred years) cliff dwelling. He spent time there trying to get a sense of place as a member of that vanished society would have felt it:

> I had gleaned, of course, no facts about my people. And for once my decision not to read up on the Canyon beforehand was a decided drawback. I did not even know the traditional uses that anthropologists had no doubt assigned by now to the different kinds of pottery.

> (Colin Fletcher, *The Man Who Walked Through Time*)

Having some basic information can allow you to see patterns in what would otherwise be simply fragmentary random elements.

I have often found while traveling that I have richer fantasies and associations about locations when I know something of their history. I am sure that those who know the story of Catharine Howard's dash down the long gallery at Hampton Court Palace in an attempt to save herself from Henry VIII's sentence of death must experience that hall differently (and more strongly) than people who do not bring that image with them.

Instant recognition can be not only a confirmation of what one already knows, but a leap forward in understanding: prior knowledge plus immediate data combine to produce a new concept of how things work or what happened there. Boyd Norton, a lover of mountain rivers, provides a moving example:

> Of all the places I've visited trying to achieve a sense of historical perspective, not many have fulfilled my expectations. . . . But perhaps my strongest feelings have been generated at this place where I now stand on the shore of the Snake River in Hell's Canyon (on the border between Oregon and Idaho). It is the spot where Chief Joseph led his people across this deep raging river, seeking escape from an oppressive United States Government.
> . . . Perhaps it is the gloom of weather, but I sense the sadness of Joseph and his people at having to leave this beloved land of theirs. From the Wallowa Valley west of here they began the long journey that would end in tragedy for them. What makes a people flee from a land that has been their home for countless generations?

> (Boyd Norton, *Rivers of the Rockies*)

Norton's moment was changed from one of just appreciating spectacular scenery to one of questioning basic social processes, because he brought some knowledge of the setting's history to that moment.

The final advantage is probably the most obvious: advance knowledge can be means of survival. The greater the potential for possible fatal mistakes, the more useful it is to have this information, and the less one can afford to learn about the setting gradually through trial and error. The Eskimo legends described earlier are not just cultural identity trips, they provide valuable information to travelers in a demanding environment that is not forgiving of missteps or lost directions. Similar advantages apply for advance images of city settings, such as knowing that certain areas have a high incidence of street crime and should be avoided at night.

Given these advantages of preformed images, there are several important limitations that should be mentioned. One of them is sometimes quite subtle: instant recognition may blind us to seeing the richness of what is actually there. We are looking so hard for what we are supposed to see that we do not allow new unexpected features to emerge. In terms of a rich immediate sense of place, this is indeed a large potential loss. When this is a strong pattern, we might as well have stayed at home and imagined the trip, which would have been much cheaper.

Another potential cost is that the advance information may be untrue or incomplete. When this is the case we may actually lose opportunities, such as not going into disreputable areas of the city that are, in fact, fairly low-risk and would provide exciting new place experiences. In the first case of accurate but rigid images, the opportunities are there but we are not able to sense them; with false information, we may not even allow the opportunities to develop. This latter cost is especially prevalent in our age of advertising, where every transportation company, tourist board, or chamber of commerce has a stake in deliberately trying to implant certain information in advance so that you will visit their setting, believe that you enjoyed it, and tell your friends about it, thus programming them in the same way you were programmed. Promotional literature is always designed to manipulate the instant recognition process toward the advertiser's vested interests.

RECOGNITION AND VALUES

There are two further points to be made. One is that perception and understanding (the basic psychological processes that relate to instant recognition) are not the only types of place experience. In particular, sheer aesthetic moments of joy, beauty, or power from experiencing new settings are valuable, and not necessarily related to preformed images. They may happen when we least expect it, with no advance preparation.

The second point is that there is no simple answer to the question of whether one *should* seek advance information and images. There is a case to be made for (a) going someplace fresh, seeing whatever is there, and then seeking more information to augment your immediate experience; and for (b) gathering some information in advance, then going to the setting better equipped to see patterns and expand on your basic perceptions while there. Which is the better strategy probably depends on several factors, including:

- The degree of risk in the new setting: the higher the risk, the more (b) is called for, unless the experience you seek is literally dealing freshly with an unknown risky situation.
- Your ability to break out of habit patterns and be aware of your stereotyped images: the higher this ability, the more it is possible to make (b) both a safe and rich experience.

Some features may be instantly recognized by one generation, but not by another: Boston's Swan Boats.

- The extent to which you want to have new, unpredictable place experiences: the more you enjoy this process, the more (a) would be useful as a general style.
- The qualities of the setting itself: I would guess that settings rich in historic events and traces of human influence provide richer experiences with pre-knowledge, (b), while striking natural environments will provide most benefit from strategy (a). Of course one needs to know something about the setting in advance in order even to choose which strategy to use.

NOTES

1. Peter Gould and Rodney White, *Mental Maps*, Harmondsworth, Middlesex: Penguin Books, 1974, pp. 130–133.
2. Kevin Lynch, *The Image of the City*, Cambridge, Mass. and London: The MIT Press, 1960, Chapter 4.
3. Stanley Milgram and Denise Jodelet, "Psychological Maps of Paris," in H. Proshansky, W. Ittelson, and L. Rivlin, *Environmental Psychology: People in their Settings* (revised ed.), New York: Holt, Rinehart and Winston, 1976.

16   Cities As Settings

The modern city as a collection of settings for people's activities has been analyzed from so many different viewpoints that few comments of a general nature would be new to many readers. The subject of city life also is vast.[1] There is nonetheless, a purpose to be served here by devoting a chapter to city settings. As the shape, pace, and climate of cities affect so many people's experiences (either constantly or periodically), city settings contribute significantly to the quality of their sense of place, whether it is positive or negative, rich or sparse, enhancing or debilitating. Cities also vary tremendously in their spirit of place, with some producing positive place experiences and others producing negative ones.

There seems to be a continuing decline in many American cities' spirit of place, and therefore decreasing quality of experiences. As a means to understanding why this would be so, I would like first to apply some of the main factors that contribute to sense of place, and then to describe identifiable trends that produce a bland, uninteresting spirit of place for both residents and visitors.

Enclosure and Surprise

Cities with twists, turns, and cul-de-sacs generate greater place awareness than those that are laid out on a regular grid that allows one to see what is ahead for many blocks. This sense is enhanced by visual barriers that create an identity for many areas around a city, as opposed to "places" that have been formally designed, such as a park or collection of government buildings. Cities that have streets that allow a pedestrian to explore both sides while walking are remembered as offering positive place experiences, because the scale is right for one to see both things and people along the way (see photo on p. 82). If there is variety to the sights, so much the better.

Patterns and Sequences

Layout and placement determine in part the experiences users have, especially their regular patterns and sequences of experience. For instance, a city that is compact, with many kinds of work, play, and residential spaces within walking distance of one another, will be well used for more hours of the day than one in which these three zones are separated by long distances, requiring some kind of transport from one to another. It is a different experience of place to be able to walk over to Harvard Square to see what's happening versus getting into your car and driving for fifteen minutes to get to the Burlington (Massachusetts) Mall. Thus Boston and Los Angeles, for example, are both cities, but the repeating patterns of their residents' experiences are totally different because one is compact and the other is very spread out.

CITY PLACE DISEASES

Given these factors, most cities will have some distinctive feel and a spirit of place that appeal to at least some of their residents and visitors. Just as some cities are particularly strong in place identity, others seem gradually (or rapidly) to be losing their individuality and capacity to stimulate responses. From the viewpoint of this book, they seem to be suffering from one or more of the following place diseases, which are eating away at their spirit and vitality.

Bank Blight

There seems to be an almost universal trend for major cities to spawn more and more banking operations, so that eventually many streets contain more of these than any other type of facility.

This causes a place disease because it usually degrades the richness of a walker's experiences. When a new branch is opened in a central city area, it has usually displaced something else, such as a shop or news stand, which had provided visually interesting facades and/or settings (not to mention items one could purchase easily, but that now must be sought in a department store).

The whole right-hand side of the street represents Insurance Insipidness, a form of Bank Blight in Boston. Not exactly a peak experience for pedestrians.

This variety contrasts with the experience of passing building after building associated with banking: little to look at in the building itself, few changes from day to day, and an active discouragement of people lingering in the vicinity (on the assumption that anyone who does this is a potential robber who is looking over the layout). In other words, the banks become blank spaces in the flow of experiences, dead areas to be passed in order to reach more interesting ones. If enough of these accumulate in the same area, its vitality is gone. People may still walk there, but only because (and when) they must, in order to accomplish some errand; when they walk for the sheer pleasure of exploration or just looking, they will go elsewhere.

A bank's attempt to soften Bank Blight's effect with window displays.

There are some exceptions to these effects. In a special section of London called the City, banks and insurance companies reflect the identity of the area and help create a strong spirit of place. When they spill out and take over other areas, however, they usually still look like they should be in the City, and this confuses the identities of other neighborhoods instead of enhancing them. Their effect is mixed: they are convenient for transient workers and tourists, and moderately so for residents, but are dull for all types of users as far as visual interest is concerned.

Why does the explosion of banks and insurance companies occur? The reasons are no doubt complex, but one of them is probably the fact that they seem to end up with most of the available cash, so that they are the most likely to expand as a means of using their excess funds. This is not a sound economic theory, but it seems to fit the pattern.

Suspended Animation

This is a more general case of the creation of dead areas in the city, of which banks were a special instance. Suspended animation usually takes the forms of urban removal, consisting of city administrators or private developers tearing down supposedly unusable structures and then leaving them as fields of rubble or craters for a number of years, because of a change in plans or a hitch in permits or funding. Sites that are a scarce resource to the residents and small businesses are thus tied and used by no one, at a very high aggregate loss to the community when they are accumulated over a number of years and locations.

Another form of suspended animation is the dead time zone—a long period of each day when a site is not used at all. This is the classic pattern of much (but not all) of the new building complexes erected in the last thirty years or so. Its prime cause is the creation of single-use facilities (such as a large office building or industrial "park") that have high peak times of use followed by long periods with no use at all. As settings, they are uninteresting, dull, and even dangerous at the empty times, as there are few observers to reduce the temptation of muggers and other predators.

By contrast, there are certain city areas that are truly animated, notable for their mixed uses and lack of dead times: Covent Garden was definitely one of these before the vegetable and flower markets were moved out. The area was alive 24 hours each day, with the market, small businesses, shops, theatres, restaurants, and residences each generating human activities with different patterns and time cycles. It was the best intensive use of a confined geographic area that I have ever seen, with the market loading area (which was most active in the 11 PM to 8 AM period) being used for theatre and restaurant parking in the evening, and for business in midmorning and afternoon. The variety of visual experiences was almost unique compared with most of today's cities. It remains to be seen whether the area can maintain this flavor of rich multiple use now that the market function has been moved out. There are probably some comparably used sites in the United States, but I do not know where they are.

Fast-Food Fungus.

Fast Food Fungus

A spreading disease of American origin, consists of a lively pedestrian precinct being filled in by establishments such as hamburger houses (McDonald's is the best known worldwide, having even spread to Champs Elysées in Paris), chicken chains such as Kentucky Fried Chicken, and pizza houses such as Pizza Hut in the United States or Pizza Express in London. Place disease occurs when a certain concentration has been reached, so that the fast food chains drive out most of the other establishments that perhaps made the area interesting. One can eat only so much MSG in an afternoon or evening, and watching others eat Big Macs is only a sometime thing as a spectator sport. People begin to desert the area, and eventually its pedestrian activity falls off to some lower, possibly moribund level, at which point a number of the eating places die out, leaving the area with a case of terminal fried chicken or fish and chips.

Exodus of Residents

There are many forces in the modern American city that drive its residents out of the central area into surrounding suburbs: rising living costs and taxes, decreasing public services, loss of residential space to higher-profit commercial redevelopment and office blocks, zoning laws and building codes that discourage residential reuse of buildings built originally for other purposes, and so on. All of these create increasingly nonresidential city centers that have no around-the-clock population.

I have called this a disease rather than just a pattern because I believe that it reduces the richness of place experiences for all city users, residents and visitors alike. Landscape architect Lawrence Halprin nicely described the positive value of central residential areas:

I know of no great and beautiful city where people do not live close to the core. For the whole quality of a city's life—its personality and its image—is set by its inhabitants, not by its merchants or its tourists or the suburbanites who live on its fringes and scatter for home with the 4:30 whistle. It is the city's dwellers who fill its streets at night, use its parks and restaurants, populate its open spaces and plazas, and in the last analysis, fight for its amenities. When the city loses its inhabitants, it will die. And it will surely die as long as it does not provide a fine well-rounded environment in which to live.

(Lawrence Halprin, *Cities*)

When the city loses its around-the-clock life, it loses its heart, and the vitality of human activities is dispersed to the surrounding suburbs. In the United States, the suburban shopping mall has played a major role in this drive, as has overdevelopment of office space. By contrast, these forces have not yet dominated in Paris, which has remained a great international city because it has kept its heart at the center.

Routing the residents from a city has a number of degrading effects on its spirit of place. Fewer and fewer people are able to experience the center at different times of day. The restaurants, theatres, and shops have a harder time surviving, as they must depend for business on transient workers who leave as soon as the workday ends, a pattern that reduces spontaneity of use. I also suspect that a city center with few residents fails in sociography: it is a poor stimulator of fantasies for visitors. Put the other way round, one of the major stimulators of visitors' fantasies in a city is the feeling of identification with the permanent residents, imagining what it would be like to be living there full-time (e.g., on San Francisco's Russian Hill or in New York's East Side or Greenwich Village areas). Fantasizing about working in various office buildings is certainly possible, but not as likely to be a regular source of fun.

Waste the Waterfront

This disease seems to be an American specialty. Historically, American cities that had ocean, lake, or riverfront structured the areas poorly in terms of possible place experiences. They were often walled-off from the residents by industry, roads, or rail lines that took no account of the value of allowing people access to watch what happened there or just enjoy the views.

From the standpoint of high-quality spirit of place, this treatment was quite costly to most of a city's users, both resident and nonresident. Waterfronts have special qualities of light, space, long views, visual variety, and recreation possibilities (boating, sunning, fishing) (see Chapter 17). Wasting them is a classic example of not capitalizing on an asset.

We can see the costs of this disease through examples of cities that have not succumbed to it: Paris with its wonderful relationship to the Seine, especially the pedestrian *quais* and the numerous bridges that allow choices of where to cross the river; London and its banks of the Thames, with such spots as Embankment Gardens near Charing Cross, or the homes along the river bank near Kew, although it also has its road-wasted and power-station stretches; and Geneva, with its miles of lakeside promenades and gardens with their unobstructed view of the lake.

To be fair, many cities in the United States have lately begun to realize the potential spirit of place of their waterfronts. New York has created its South Street Seaport Area; San Francisco has a history of redeveloping (for festive use by both residents and visitors) its waterfront, and finally stopped building the Embarcadero elevated expressway in midair to prevent it from sealing off the waterfront any more than it had already done. The city of San Antonio, Texas has created a highly publicized riverfront park in a city that had always turned its back on the area. My favorite example is, of course, my own home city of Boston, with its new expansive waterfront park that contains gardens, play areas, benches, arbors, and infinite opportunities for people to watch boats, the harbor, and one another. The park has been heavily used since it opened, and the whole area has come alive, with many wharf buildings being recycled for commercial and residential uses.

This area fits many of the criteria used in this book to define a strong spirit of place. It has a mix of old and new buildings, in scale with one another, which are good stimulators of fantasies. It has residential, commercial, and office facilities mixed together, so patterns of use are not one-sided. There are facilities for doers and plenty of spots for watchers. The views of the harbor and back to the historic Quincy Market area of the city are both interesting and contribute to a strong sense of identity—you can tell where you are. There are elements of surprise as you explore a new wharf area, finding a modern furniture showroom or an old weatherbeaten structure that calls up images of nineteenth century fishing fleets. All in all, it makes real sense as a city place.

Boston's Waterfront Park is an attempt to reverse Waste the Waterfront.

SOME POSSIBLE ANTIDOTES

The conditions that were sampled here are some of the more obvious ways in which the spirit of place erodes in a city. There are presumably many other creeping processes that lower the quality of city place experiences, and readers may have their own examples that are particularly irritating to them. I would hope that many readers might be moved to pass observations on to local governments and others involved in influencing such processes, such as developers, designers, and influential journalists.[2] The results of such feedback might be interesting. As everybody becomes more aware of the loss of such experiences as the micro-world, personal places, and rich fantasies, they might begin to express higher expectations to the people and institutions who influence the fabric of their city.

This could lead to a new classification system for labeling population centers, based not on size of population (e.g., village, town, city, and megalopolis), but on the spirit of place there. Only cities that tended to provide high-quality place experiences would maintain the label "city." As an urban area becomes more homogenized, less residential, more monumental and segmented in terms of uses and time structures, it should have its "city" label revoked, and some other one applied to it, one that was more descriptive of the kind of place experience it provided for its users.

Attempts have been made to rate the quality of life in American cities using mainly economic indicators (probably because they provide quantitative measures). This could be extended by using our place dimensions to rate these areas, and providing new names for different profiles of settings. For instance, a center consisting mainly of offices and supporting services, and which tended to be deserted after work hours, might be called a "busiplex." A large, diffuse area with no residential center and loosely joined neighborhoods would be an "urbanus," or a "mallurbus" if shopping malls were prominent features of the region. A population center that consisted mainly of services that were supporting one another, that had a declining residential population, and generally low visual interest could be called a "circoplex"; while one that had been "renewed" into large-scale towers and blocks with little of interest for pedestrians to see and do, organized around parking for cars, could be an "auto-monumentus."

As you can see, the alternative names are not that good. They are difficult to generate because we do not yet have a good common vocabulary for place experiences. Even so, it is still worth the effort to try to judge city settings in terms of quality, not just square miles or density per acre. The ratings might even be started by some private or quasiprivate groups that compiled a city guide like the Michelin guide, and rated cities (or busiplexes) with a star system. This would make trends in changes of city settings visible sooner and increase the possibility of quick government or private action to reverse the diseases. Development decisions and licensing approvals could be made on the basis of the balance of settings in an area and what the proposed alteration would do to tip the balance. The city council of Cambridge, Massachusetts, applied just such a test several years ago when they announced a moratorium on licenses for fast-food establishments in Harvard Square.

THE SHORT-TERM EFFECTS OF THE SENSE OF PLACE

Finally, we also have an immediate opportunity to apply our awareness of city settings, through our choices of where to live and to do things. If you are experiencing your city as dull, overbearing, visually chaotic, or lacking in fantasy material, maybe it is time to consider moving on, even if it represents a risk. The risk of *not* moving is a hidden one, but it is no less real: a cumulative pattern of poor place experiences in a life that is, like everyone's, limited in time and opportunity.

NOTES

1. A few of the better analyses of city settings include:

   Brent C. Brolin, *Architecture in Context: Fitting New Buildings with Old*, New York: Van Nostrand Reinhold, 1980;

   Gordon Cullen, *The Concise Townscape*, London: The Architectural Press, 1961 (paperback, 1971);

   Leonard Duhl, *The Urban Condition: People and Policy in the Metropolis*, New York: Basic Books, 1963;

   Lawrence Halprin, *Cities*, Cambridge, Mass. and London: The MIT Press, 1973;

   Jane Jacobs, *The Death and Life of Great American Cities*, New York: Vintage Books, 1961;

   Kevin Lynch, *The Image of the City*, Cambridge, Mass. and London: The MIT Press, 1960;

   Charles Mercer, *Living in Cities: Psychology and the Urban Environment*, Harmondsworth, Middlesex: Penguin Books, 1975;

   Lewis Mumford, *The City of History*, New York: Harcourt, Brace and World, 1961;

   Mary Proctor and Bill Matuszeski, *Gritty Cities*, Philadelphia: Temple University Press, 1978.

2. One of my favorites is Ada Louise Huxtable, the former *New York Times* architecture critic. For instance, readers can learn much about city diseases by reading her collection of lively essays, *Will They Ever Finish Bruckner Boulevard?* (New York: Macmillan; London: Collier-Macmillan, Ltd., 1971).

PART SIX

IMPROVING OUR SENSE OF PLACE

17

A Smear of Green: Becoming Better Users of Settings

When current critics have complained about bad or degrading place experiences in American society, they have placed the blame heavily on negative aspects of settings: noise, air, and water pollution, bland design, inhuman scale, lack of connection with history, and so on.

One of the basic themes of this book, however, has been the assumption that improvements in our sense of place can come from the sociophysical settings themselves, or the ways in which we perceive and use our settings, or both. This chapter will consider opportunities for improving our own patterns of using settings, and the following one is concerned with the issue of how to create settings with a richer spirit of place. The main concepts that facilitate better use of settings include choosing locations, exuberant use, seizing opportunities, and pattern management.

CHOOSING LOCATIONS

A key influence over how well a person uses a setting begins with the original choice of that setting versus some other. If an inappropriate location is chosen, subsequent attempts to use it as effectively as possible are always uphill battles. Considerable energy and frustration could be saved by putting more conscious energy and effort into choices about where to do different activities, so that the hows can be done more easily, with more zest. This process would contrast with many of our location choices that are made unconsciously, being influenced by chance factors such as where we happen to be at a particular moment.[1]

Matching

One issue is the degree to which one can match expected activities to the qualities of a particular setting. Matching should be used for a variety of location decisions, such as where to live, work, perform certain tasks, play or relax, and visit. Being more conscious of which activities are most important in a particular situation can improve the matching process considerably, and lead to a more satisfying sense of place.

Farley Mowat provides a nice example of the matching process in his analysis of why a group of Eskimos had chosen a particular location for their village:

> After I had begun to master the problem of communication, one of the first questions I put to Ootek was to ask why the Little Hills area had been singled out from an apparently similar, but almost limitless, expanse of plains to be the home of the Ihalmiut. . . .
> To begin with, Ootek gave me to understand that the selection of any permanent campsite is based primarily on three major considerations. The first is: "Will the deer, who are our life, approve?" Or, in direct terms, will the site provide the supply of meat which is essential to human life?

Using a well-designed Bay Area Rapid Transit station court for an outdoor walking seminar.

IMPROVING OUR SENSE OF PLACE

The next major consideration is that of a fuel supply. In this part of the Arctic where animals cannot supply fat-fuel for cooking and for heat, the camps must be placed within reach of a good supply of the dwarf shrubs of the Barrens.

The third and most complex factor in the choice of a camp is concerned with the proximity of the dead, for it is not wise to build igloos or tents in a place where there are many graves.

(Farley Mowat, *People of the Deer*)

Thus in functional terms, the village site is chosen primarily for shelter and survival (food and fuel) and one symbolic reason (propitious relations with the dead).

In modern urban cultures, choosing a location is often quite complex, and the consequences of bad matching take longer to become visible than they do in the Barrens. There are, nonetheless, real costs to bad matches. For instance, when people think about possible new areas in which to live, they will sometimes choose a setting in which they have enjoyed holiday experiences, thereby loading the choice heavily on fun they have had. Unfortunately, the process of residing full-time in an area usually requires a greater balance of functions, including security, social contact, and good work settings. A poor match leads to unexpected dissatisfaction and a different sense of place than when recreation was the only concern.

In terms of matching activities to settings, there is a problem of "symbolic congruence": that is, the extent to which a chosen setting fits the basic message a person or group is trying to communicate by doing the activity in the first place. For example, when planning a conference on the problems of urban sprawl and unchecked development, it would probably be best to choose a location that represented sensible land-use policies, or to hold it right in the middle of some area of runaway growth, if part of the design of the conference were to use the immediate setting as a case example. The worst alternative would be to hold the conference in the out-of-control area and say nothing about the site. This would at least raise a question in many participants' minds whether their conclusions would make any difference whatsoever.

Special Settings for Special Events

A second aspect of choosing settings concerns short-term occasions: where to hold special, one-time events. Many decisions about locations are based on criteria that are usually assumptions: lowest cost, easiest to arrange, most available, easiest access. These criteria obscure the one measure that should appear first in the equation: will the setting provide an appropriate, rich place experience that enhances the original purpose for having the event? If it does not, then the event wastes a potential resource, even though it may save money. (Following this criterion, the perfect event would be one that was not held at all, thus saving the whole cost.)

A few examples should make this simple concept clear. Construction crews working on high-rise buildings have traditionally held a "topping-off" ceremony when the structural frame has reached its final height. This ceremony is usually held in the most symbolically powerful setting—the top of the building—rather than in a hotel banquet room (which would be a more comfortable, but irrelevant, site). It was once suggested to the board of directors of a troubled railroad that they have one of their frequent "crisis" meetings in the dingy waiting room of one of their stations, so that they would become more attuned to the experiences and problems of their passengers. Whether the site is glamorous or squalid, it can serve the purpose if it is well-chosen, giving the addition of a symbolic dimension to an event.

Kevin Lynch has suggested that a rich use of place possibilities should also include the mirror image of the above examples: special events for special sites, particularly at those times when sites are undergoing transition:

> Since, as I have argued, the destruction and death of an environment may be as significant a point in its process as its creation, why not celebrate that moment in some more significant way? . . . There could be a visible event and a suitable transformation when a place 'came of age' or was about to disappear. We concentrate on inauguration so singlemindedly. But there was a famous party in the Florentine ghetto just before it was cleared away. . . . With a little stage management, the wrecking of buildings could also be turned into a public spectacle, an occasion of awe, of excitement, or of curiosity satisfied by a sight of what's inside.

> (Kevin Lynch, *What Time Is This Place?*)

Using temporary sites: the "Chinese Garden" in London's Covent Garden area (site has since been built on).

IMPROVING OUR SENSE OF PLACE

Staying Versus Moving On

The other major location decision is whether to remain where we are living, working, or playing, or to move to a new location. Although this is an implicit choice that is always present, many people become rooted in one place and assume that because they are there, it must be the right one. This is, of course, not necessarily so; all one knows automatically about the present setting is that it is where one is at the present. Thus another means of using settings well is periodically to ask the question of whether the advantages of the present one have been dwindling. Many people ask this too infrequently, and miss a considerable amount of stimulating place experience by moving later than they should have. One reason for this is that they become resigned to what they get from a site, and forget that they could expect more. They only rediscover this when they do finally move on.

EXUBERANT USE

Exuberant use is based on the assumption that you will have richer place experiences if you are personally free or loose enough to use a setting in lively ways, and not be limited just to traditional or socially acceptable ones. The emphasis is on allowing yourself to be innovative, deviant, or playful in using various qualities of a setting.

Loosening Constraints

The most consistent blocks to exuberant use are probably personal ones: the combination of perceptions, expectations, assumptions, habits, social concerns, and personal fears that keep us from using everything a setting provides. A nice example was described by Edward Abbey, who was looking for a way to descend a steep mountain snowfield that had just required two hours to climb. He made a few preliminary tests and then rode a flat rock down the snowfield like a sled, requiring only a few minutes. It was an unusual move that provided a great experience for him, and was done in spite of his fears, not because he had none.[2]

Social constraints also block exuberant use in the form of our perceptions of what others expect us to do. Our view of these expectations may or may not be accurate, but if we believe them and care about living up to them, they reduce the amount of freedom with which we could use our settings. For instance, many writers have noted the pattern of families using their homes in ways that will look acceptable to neighbors, rather than in ways that would allow them to use their resources best. It has also been seen that we take on an increasingly large set of expectations about "proper" behavior as we grow from children to adults, which causes the gap between exuberant use of settings by children and the relatively constricted use by adults. As adults, we are also often dressed wrong for spontaneous activities such as tramping along an inviting but muddy footpath. This is a social constraint in a sense, as

Rules or no rules, the day and spot (Boston's Public Garden) demand lying about on the grass.

it usually hinges on a learned feeling that it would not be "right" to muddy our shoes or soil a suit.

Taking Trouble

Some of the exuberant uses we miss are lost not because of an active constraint, but because of a passive one: we do not take the trouble to do something that would add significantly to our experiences. There are many times when we need to take extra trouble, to make an extra investment, in order to fulfill our basic reason for being in a setting to begin with. Getting out early in the morning to see a sunrise can be just such a rewarding experience, sensing the increasing pulse and rhythm of the world awakening—*if* we have bothered to get out of a warm bed when we could easily sleep another two hours. In order really to know your city, you need to experience it over a range of times of day, including those that are inconvenient or take extra energy. A city street at 3 AM is a world unlike any we see in daytime, and well worth experiencing occasionally just for its own sake.

Physical exertions are often assumed to be distasteful or too difficult, and one's place experiences are thereby narrowed. For instance, physically fit people who choose only to visit sites that are accessible by car have unnecessarily closed themselves out of many of the most exciting places in the United States: all those beautiful wilderness areas that do not happen to have roads leading to them. Not only are the sites beautiful, but the absence of cars makes them even more rewarding if one has made the effort to get there.

Another opportunity to be rewarded for taking trouble occurs when you are visiting a city, wilderness, or house that has a "best" approach that

shows it off well. It is often well worth making a special effort to approach it correctly.

Clearing Yourself

In order to use settings exuberantly, it is sometimes necessary to clear out of our minds competing concerns or activities. There is a Buddhist saying that captures the notion well: "When you eat, eat, when you sleep, sleep." In other words, high-quality place experiences can be obtained by focusing on a particular activity and clearing others away. Self-clearing contrasts with a prevalent style in modern industrial society, which is to do three or four things at once (e.g., visit a cathedral, think about a business problem, and plan the next segment of your trip) and none of them well. This multiple activity often neutralizes the experience of the setting, so that you are never really there and experiencing it fully.

One simple method for clearing and focusing yourself is to shut your eyes and try to visualize the details of your immediate surroundings. When you open your eyes and check your mind's picture, you begin to see elements that had been invisible before, and at that moment you are truly there. Another simple clearing method is to ask yourself, "Why am I here at this moment, rather than being anywhere else in the world?" If you really think about this question, a number of the activities competing in your head become obviously extraneous.

The clearing concept illustrates the point that exuberant use does not necessarily mean loud or boisterous use. It may also be the quiet, contemplative, focused use of a place's best feature at a particular moment, such as when a hiker chooses not to build a fire on a starlit night in the Rockies, and thus not be cut off from the total experience and feel of the night.

Recharging

Recharging oneself means using settings as stimulation for new ideas, energy, outlooks on life, or whatever. My favorite example is the poor man who lived in the Bowery on New York's Lower East Side. Periodically he would save up enough money to take a room at the Plaza Hotel uptown; then he would return to his regular haunts. He obviously felt that the periodic place experiences of great contrast to his usual life style were worth much more than spreading out his money to improve his day-to-day life ever so (probably unnoticeably) slightly.

When travel experiences are used well, they serve this recharging function. Our experiences in temporary settings suggest new ways to use our permanent locations; or they spark new interests that we can then follow at a more leisurely pace. When travel is done without an awareness of the value of recharging, however, it can be reduced to the mechanics of getting from place to place (such as setting rigid driving schedules so that all the planned points are covered according to plan) and often results in a net energy drain rather than gain.

USING OPPORTUNITIES

One of the key qualities that distinguishes place people from non–place people is the extent to which the former consistently take advantage of the opportunities offered by their settings. They recognize that often a particular setting is better at providing certain opportunities (for activities, sights, experiences, stimulation) than any other. There are usually several uses that would feel right in such a plan; a person who seizes special opportunities is the one who uses it for things that could not be done elsewhere.

For instance, a friend described to me in a letter an interesting incident:

> When I was a student I spent a prolonged holiday in Tuscany and Umbria. One stupefying day I walked from Perugia to Assisi (7 or 8 miles). In Assisi, which is topographically and architecturally a most remarkable place, I visited the great basilica of San Francisco. Approaching the building across an open area I was astonished to find, lolling amidst the long grass reading Ian Fleming, a friend from Edinburgh. He said, "What are you doing here?" I replied, "I've come to visit the basilica." "What's that?" he said.

The reader in the grass may well have been enjoying himself immensely, but he was not operating in what we would call a mode of seizing opportunities.

On the positive side: when riding a train through new territory, the special opportunity is to look at the passing countryside. By contrast, many people choose to read, do puzzles, or other things to pass the time, while the chance to see what is there literally passes them by. Again, this is not to say that reading or playing games are bad things to do, only that they do not take advantage of the train's route through unknown settings. I am not suggesting that we always have to use the special features of a setting, but only that we should ask, "What are the opportunities here?" so that we make a more informed choice and know what we are giving up if we do not focus on them.

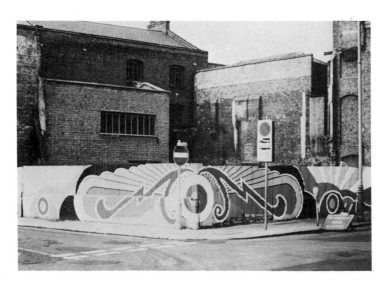

Using fences as opportunities.

IMPROVING OUR SENSE OF PLACE

Amplification

I am not talking about any particular behavior being good or bad, but rather am emphasizing the choice of a particular behavior in a particular setting. Thus we can also use reading as a positive strategy; the key is in the choice of what to read. When visiting a particular setting, such as a new city, one can amplify place experience by reading material (fiction, history, travel literature) that relates to where one is, so that perceptions and ideas from reading play off of one another and make both experiences richer:

> One of my own special pleasures is to read novels while in the locale they describe. I walked the streets of Halifax one snowladen February day with Hugh MacLennan's *Barometer Rising* in my hand. . . . Henry Fauconnier's *Soul of Malaya* came alive to me while I was sitting in the shade of a rubber plantation that looked out across his House of Palms, now reconstructed after it was destroyed by the Japanese, a home Fauconnier built in Selangor.
>
> (Robin Winks, *The Historian as Detective*)

A little foresight would allow us to pick up a few books about or set in the new locale, so that we focus our attention on the place and its features. Such reading suggests new things to notice, new moods to acknowledge, which would not be possible if our reading materials were selected with no thought to where they would be read.

Tuning In

One reason people do not use opportunities is that they do not do well at tuning in to their immediate surroundings. For the reasons we described in Chapters 3 and 4, some people have real difficulty being fully aware of their present context and its possibilities. Here is a near-perfect example:

> A feeling for the lay and character of the land must have been near-universal in the ancient Mediterranean world . . . . But my friend from New York, an excellent abstract artist, walks through our Berkshire woods smoking Gauloises and talking of Berlin. It is too bad he cannot be where he is, enjoying the glades and closures, the climbs, the descents, the flat stretches strewn with Canada Mayflower and Wintergreen. . . . "Forgive me," he says. . . . "To me, this is all a smear of green." And so he walks along in an envelope of smoke and talk.
>
> (Richard Wilbur, "The Writer's Sense of Place," *South Dakota Review*, Vol. 13, Autumn, 1975)

The image is appropriate, for tuned-out people carry their own environments around with them as shells, avoiding any recognition of worthwhile qualities in new or different settings.

I would simply suggest that one who can tune in to where one is at the present moment, regardless of wishes to the contrary, is more likely to use opportunities in, and have a sense of, place that on the average is richer than can one who does not tune in well. Many methods for doing this have been developed by the late Fritz Perls and other Gestalt therapists, and I would recommend their work to those who would like to develop the skill.[3]

Characteristic Seasons

An obvious feature of settings that contains potential opportunities is weather. Special activities can be enjoyed in areas with distinctive climates, such as the Mediterranean's sunshine or the Alps' snowfalls. What is not so obvious is that many people spend most of their lives avoiding these opportunities, especially when the activities cannot be performed in the kind of weather they prefer. By having favorite weather types they radically narrow their range of place experiences.

By contrast, James Drawbell wrote in his memoir of Scotland that he had decided to try to take advantage of a geographic location's most characteristic season, so that he would come to know it in its strongest character, rather than at its blandest.[4] The bland experience comes with retreating from all the extremes—leaving the north in winter, and avoiding the southern climes in summer. The result may be physically not uncomfortable, but it also is less stimulating in terms of place experiences; a person who has only seen Florida in the winter and Minnesota in the summer has not experienced the full depth of spirit of either setting.

Innovative Uses

People who regularly use a setting's opportunities also think of innovative uses for them. They perceive the basic qualities of the setting and then consider what special things could be done there, rather than just using stereotyped categories of activities. For example, the various rooms in a house often have special qualities: different shapes, more or less natural light, different access to the outside, and so on. Yet these features are often unused, because the rooms have been given labels such as "dining room" or "bedroom," leading people to use them in only one way. I know of only one family that has truly removed this block: they have used every room (except the bathroom) of their London flat for different functions, including moving the cooking activities from one room to another.

Children are also able to break through socially determined labels for settings, because they do not know or do not care about labels. My one-year-old nephew was given a "Busy Box" with birds and figures hanging from it for him to play with. He kept busiest by pulling off and playing with the stick that held these figures, a use of an inherent opportunity that was there, but not one that an adult (especially the makers of the Busy Box) would have been likely to recognize.

A business school program that is run by New York's Adelphi University on the commuter trains of the Long Island Railroad used the fact that commuters were stuck in temporarily fixed locations within rail cars and compact physical spaces to provide them with a self-development opportunity.[4] The general point is that we are more likely to recognize opportunities if we think about what could be done well in a setting, rather than about what has been traditionally done there or what social norms say should be done there.

IMPROVING OUR SENSE OF PLACE

Seeing possibilities and qualities in "abandoned" facilities: Seattle's Gasworks Park.

How not to use a setting: Boston's Charles River Esplanade the day after the July 4, 1976 celebration.

3. For example, see the classic *Gestalt Therapy*, by Fritz Perls, Ralph Hefferline, and Paul Goodman, (New York: Delta, 1951).

4. See James Drawbell, *Scotland Bittersweet* (London: James Macdonald & Co., Ltd., 1972, p. 33).

5. Daniel Yergin, "Business School: The Running Scout," *The American Way* (American Airlines Magazine), August 1976, p. 19.

18 Making Places by Influencing Settings

The other main approach to improving our sense of place is improving the quality of the settings themselves, making better places by enhancing their spirit of place. Conversely, we also run the risk (and often the actual effect) of reducing the quality of settings, so that they are less likely to provide rich place experiences. I will use the dimensions already discussed to suggest some ways to make better settings (through creating new ones or improving old ones) and some ways to avoid "unmaking" high-quality settings and turning them into neutral or negative situations.

CRITERIA FOR MAKING BETTER SETTINGS

The first step is to become clear in our own minds about criteria to predict that a setting will or will not be a stimulator of place experiences. The earlier chapters have suggested a number of these that we can use as guidelines.

Choices and Options

A special spirit of place exists in those settings that provide options about how they can be used. Having choice and variety in one's experiences serves a fundamental human need, and people will often choose a plain setting they can influence over a more elegant one that is fixed and unalterable.

One of the features that makes London such a good city for walkers is that its street pattern is so irregular and complex. This is not as some might think, an "inefficient" layout and waste of resources, but a richness of place, as repeated trips do not have to be routine, unchanging experiences.

Reinforcing Patterns and Sequences

Settings that provide sequences of experiences that build on one another are more likely to produce high-quality place experiences than are those that promote conflicting patterns and sequences. A low-quality example is a sports facility with poorly designed entrances and exits, so that the processes of arriving and leaving are bad enough to cancel out the joy of the actual event. A positive example is a hospital in Bern, Switzerland in which the checking-in facilities and procedures are so supportive and effective at orienting a patient that the experience takes on new, less threatening meaning.

Rich Material for Fantasies and Memories

Settings that contain many coherent cues that trigger off memories and fantasies will be more likely to provide rich place experiences than will those settings that have few cues. The actual content of the "coherent cues" will vary with the nature and history of the users: a setting that is productive for one type of person may be relatively unstimulating to another.

A Sense of Identity

A setting that has some consistent themes to its form, materials, items, arrangements, and symbolism will be more likely to produce positive place experiences than one with no thread of identity. A common complaint about many rapidly growing United States suburban areas is that they lack any geographic or regional identity, are homogeneous and bland, and therefore are not stimulating in terms of spirit of place for either residents or visitors. This trend is becoming an international malaise as building methods, materials, and styles become more and more standardized.

Highlighting Personal Awareness

Some settings have a strong spirit of place explicitly because of the new perceptions or awareness they stimulate. An example is the special Zen contemplation garden of Ryoan-Ji in Japan, where the impact on a visitor's sense of self is so great that the setting's personality is potently communicated.[1] This

IMPROVING OUR SENSE OF PLACE

is really a joint sociophysical effect, of course, as the impact is also a product of the user knowing cultural context of such a setting, and its intended uses for human psychic renewal.

Highlighting Opportunities

In line with the concepts in the previous chapter, a setting whose special features are visible is more likely, on the average, to stimulate use of those features than is one where they are more hidden. For instance, a city whose social setting includes organizations designed to inform people of entertainment, work, shopping, architectural, and other features is likely to be a rich place experience for visitors or new residents. Another city with similar resources that are not visible or accessible except to "insiders" who have lived there a long time and are connected to the right informal networks, will feel like less of a place to outsiders.

Appropriate Scale

A more subtle criterion of quality settings is the interplay of scale among its elements. The scale can be quite grand, as with the impact of the sheer size of the Grand Canyon in the United States; or it can be intimate and scaled for individual humans, such as the small pedestrian way called Bow Lane near St. Paul's in London (see photo on p. 82). The point is not the natural superiority of any particular size, but rather that a positive spirit of place comes partly through appropriate size relationships of elements to one another and to users. This is the opposite effect of that of many huge buildings built recently, such as New York's World Trade Center, where the size is so large compared to its surroundings that users can hardly relate to the setting at all.

The international terminal arrival hall at Boston's Logan Airport: creating a festive public space that plays a very important part in visitors' experience of the U.S. because it is their first contact.

Active Vitality

As described in Chapter 7, a setting's special spirit can be generated by the patterns of users' activities. They can generate a visible vitality, which those people experience and which they create for one another. Certain areas of a city become revitalized from time to time, which usually means much more than just being physically improved: it means that more people are using the area in more ways, and that they draw still others to it.

METHODS OF MAKING PLACES

Given that these are some key qualities that we would seek to create or preserve in settings, how would we go about doing this, both individually and collectively? This question really rates a book all to itself, and many have been written about it.[2] In my limited space I would like to focus on methods that follow from the previous discussions in this book; it is hoped that these will stimulate readers to think about their own potential for influencing the spirit of place in their settings. The suggestions are grouped into four strategies: creating new settings; remaking existing settings; making personal places; and not unmaking settings that already have a strong spirit of place.

Creating New Settings

Site Choices   One of the most crucial aspects of creating new settings is the choice of site. In general, I think that as our technological capabilities have expanded, the need for paying careful attention to site selection has contracted, so that we now build structures that work technically but have very little spirit of place to them—they could be anywhere. A good example is the all-glass John Hancock Tower which was built in Boston's brick Victorian Back Bay area: a lovely building that bears little relation to its equally lovely surroundings, and instead works against the scale of its site and destroys existing relationships of buildings, streets, and open space in Copley Square. It also created new, rather violent wind patterns that make some of its nearby streets almost unwalkable on certain days.

New England farm families traditionally placed their barns in special locations, often back up against a bank or hill so that they were both protected from the north wind and able to be entered with wagons at different levels. Newer materials have reduced the need for this care, and the barns built today show a resultant lack of relationship to their location. The Chinese have always considered site to be crucial to the creation of a setting with a special successful spirit of place, and the profession of geomancy (or the art and science of land divination) is still used in making choices for buildings.[1] I believe that this concern will have to be revived in Western civilization, as space and resources shrink and our technologies reach the limits of their effectiveness.

The John Hancock Tower in
Boston.

Designing for Human Needs   Although it may seem obvious, most settings are theoretically designed for human use (even zoos, where the circula-
tion of observers and staff is an important consideration). In practice, however, settings are often created to fulfill various abstract goals or needs of the
designers/developers, with little attention paid to the actual needs of potential
or known users. I think of this approach as reflecting the "modelboard mental-
ity," and it is exemplified by such projects as Brasilia (the new capital of Brazil,
which is totally out of human scale) and the City Hall Plaza in Boston, where a
large open space must have looked wonderful on sculptural models, but is
almost uninhabitable in the extremes of winter wind and summer sun. Edward
Relph has described such creations as "other-directed architecture," built for
outsiders, visitors, or other architects to marvel at, but not built to make high-
quality places for users.[2]

For housing projects, designing should include not only needs for shelter
and security, but also for social contact and activities to structure one's time.
Most low-income housing clusters are built without activity areas, on the
assumption that these are "luxuries," whereas I think that they are necessities
for all ages; the lack of settings for doing things will result in antisocial behavior in the young, boredom in the middle-aged, and disintegration and depres-
sion in the elderly.

Connected Growth   If we look at the impact of collections of buildings, I would say that in terms of spirit of place, the least effective are those where new parts have been created with no concern for how they will relate to the existing ones; more effective are those that have been masterplanned as a whole; and the most effective are those created by connected growth, evolving over time, with the new parts being carefully related to the existing ones. Many of the most engaging medieval towns are products of the last process.

A recent example is the Brattle Street area near Harvard Square in Cambridge, Massachusetts. A dense, complex arrangement of offices, shops, restaurants, paths, and covered walk-ways has grown through modifications by different developers and architects, adding up to a very special setting. The key qualities of the area are that it is connected, and that it speaks of growth, or as one architecture critic described it:

> It's an open-ended, aggregating kind of design . . . something you feel isn't quite finished, that's open to change and participation—a feeling you seldom get in any environment designed all by a single mind, the kind of environment which is essentially someone else's self-expression leaving you with only two roles to choose from: intruder or piece of the stage set.
>
> (Robert Campbell, "Piecemeal Perfection," *Boston Globe,* June 15, 1975)

Occasionally, however, a complete setting is designed in such a way that it seems to have grown up over time. A few Victorian architects in England built houses that were composed of mixed materials to look as if they had been added to in stages over several hundred years.[3] This was a spurious history, but it created some settings that still had interesting qualities of place, no matter how they evolved. If we attempt to promote connected growth, we can avoid both the lack of identity of disconnected parts and the sterility of one-shot, all-done master plans that create settings that should be places, but which are not, for most users.[4]

Building-in Flexibility   This is absolutely crucial to successful settings in a world of increasing change and decreasing natural resources. Cultural and social forces are changing rapidly, and we therefore can no longer build on the assumption that settings will be used indefinitely by the same institution with the same social structure. Nor do we have the resources to build separate settings for all our varied activities; we must create multiple-use constructions whose form and function can be altered relatively quickly and cheaply. One example is the open office with modular furniture, where both individual offices and overall layouts can be moved as tasks and organization structures change.

A functional approach to designed flexibility is the one proposed by English designer Francis Duffy, who suggests that we seek differential degrees of permanence and flexibility for different aspects of a work place: the shell of a building, which is relatively fixed and may have a useful life of 40 years; the scenery (major interior design features, color schemes, locations of walls) that may have an average life of seven years or so; and the sets, or specific arrangements, which can be made up of components that can be moved or rearranged at whatever intervals suit users' needs.[5]

This sort of flexibility has its historic counterpart in other cultures, such as the African Ik tribe, where hostile and unstable social relationships result in relatively temporary houses with variable entrance schemes that allow for quick realignment (making access easier or more difficult) as these relationships change.[6]

Incorporating Fragments   When creating a new setting, an interesting means of tying that setting to some specific time, location, and function is to incorporate relevant fragments from the historic uses of the site. The clearest statement of the possibilities inherent in the use of fragments has been made by Kevin Lynch:

> Where old structures cannot support present functions without impairing those functions, and unless they are of exceptional didactic or aesthetic value, they can be cleared away, although their fragments may be used to enhance new buildings. We need not be so concerned about perfect conformity to past form but ought rather to seek to use remains to enhance the complexity and significance of the present scene. The contrast of old and new, the accumulated concentration of the most significant elements of the various periods gone by, even if they are only fragmentary reminders of them, will in time produce a landscape whose depth no one period can equal, although such time-deep areas may be achieved only in some parts of the city.

(Kevin Lynch, What Time Is This Place?)

Incorporating fragments: the "Tower" Condominium in Cambridge, Mass.

Social System Designs   All of the previous examples have emphasized the creation of spirited physical settings. The other option is also available to us: to establish a spirited sense of place through new social norms, rules, policies, or structures so that people both use settings differently and relate to one another in new ways.

In many cases, social intervention is not only useful, it is necessary if new physical designs are actually to affect place experiences. If you design a new type of school, there will have to be accompanying changes in the teaching methods of the staff if the potential of the design is to be fulfilled. A similar need exists in new work spaces, where old policies and rules of use can keep workers from taking advantage of the new facilities. For instance, to be a really new setting, an open office design must have some changed rules and norms that allow experimentation and exuberant use, as well as control unwanted intrusions that occur more easily when walls and doors are removed. Similarly, it has been suggested that a means to a better sense of place for residents of crowded ghetto apartments is the establishment of better social norms about territoriality, intrusion, and mixed uses for single rooms.[7]

Localized Names   As noted in the chapter on instant recognition, names of settings, if they are related to something significant, can contribute to a special spirit of place. Names can take on a stimulating role by tying the present to the past and heightening perceptions of special features. In some instances, the names themselves can become separate "places," as in the case of the displaced Masai tribe in Africa, who take the names of hills, plains, and rivers with them when they relocate, thus carrying their cut roots with them.[8]

Unfortunately, the trend in the United States today seems to be in just the opposite direction. More and more names for new places have no connection with any features or historic events in the area, and could just as well be used anywhere. Many builders of housing developments choose street names based on market research into "popular" names, which means that the names tend to be the same: "Meadowbrook Road," "Parkwood Drive," "Briarwood Lane," "Forest Court," "Lakeside Place," "Spring Street," and so on. They convey no sense of place, other than being nonthreatening symbols.

We also create places by giving special, personal names to locales that have meaning to us because of special events that happened there. Thus a small dingy backstreet may become known as "Poco's Alley" in honor of the family cat's love for wandering there; or "Hurricane Bridge" marks the refuge taken in a particularly violent rainstorm. Giving these names helps us remember and see the places as something special, thereby providing an extra layer of meaning to our place experiences.

Reworking Existing Settings

Besides creating new settings, we have the opportunities to enhance the spirit of place of existing ones. I would like to suggest several illustrative methods that can help.

Rehabilitation and/or Reuse   In the last few years, due in part to materials shortage, there has been a strong upsurge in interest on the part of developers and designers in the renovation and reuse of existing structures, rather than more typical wholesale pulling down and starting from scratch. Sometimes the settings are improved for their current function, as when substandard housing is upgraded to meet new requirements of shelter and security; sometimes the setting is altered to fit entirely new uses: factories into housing or shops, housing into offices or gallery spaces, and so on.[9] Both rehabilitation and reuse can produce an exciting spirit of place if designers can take advantage of the more exciting features of the older setting, rather than wiping them out in the name of "improvements." For example, Ghirardelli Square is an exciting complex of shops and restaurants created from an old San Francisco waterfront chocolate factory. Part of its excitement is the complexity of levels, passages, and spaces that provide continual surprise and choice to the pedestrian. The designers could have simplified the internal structure, keeping only the outer shell, but they chose to elaborate the complexity suggested by different areas of the old working factory, thus achieving a much richer variety of views and surprises.

At a larger scale, leaders in many United States towns have only recently begun to see their down-at-heel Main Street shopping precincts as potential resources that can be brought back to viable town centers. The emphasis here has often been on undoing earlier mistakes in renovation, such as removing the gaudy storefront veneers that were pasted on as symbols of "modernism" in the 1940s and 1950s. Special places can often be created simply by reemphasizing some of the best (but subsequently hidden) features of the original buildings.[10]

Festive reuse of the complexity of an existing setting: Ghirardelli Square in San Francisco, a marketplace made from a chocolate factory.

The danger in the renovation of a Main Street or similar space is the temptation to create a reproduction of an earlier era, rather than a precinct fit for modern uses but with its forms and past messages intact for stimulating memories and fantasies. The trick is not to try literally to recreate the past, with a museum-like reconstruction, but to use quality buildings from past eras and maintain their best features while adapting them to economic uses in the present.

All in all, the effort to reestablish the basic quality of older buildings seems to me to be a relatively high-return, conservation-oriented means of enhancing place experiences in cities and towns. The basic assumption is quite sound: we are more likely to create a high-quality setting by using the accumulated traces of a site's history, and by affecting whole groups of buildings (and precincts in a city) than we are by remodeling single buildings that bear little relationship to their surroundings.

Diagnosis and Tinkering   This approach is not concerned with qualities of old buildings, but with the problems of a particular setting and the way they negate a spirit of place. The approach is simply (1) to ask diagnostic questions using the kinds of dimensions we have explored in this book: what detracts from the identity of this setting as a special place?; which elements generate fantasies, which do not?; why might people feel unconnected with this setting?; and (2) to work with the setting to correct the basic flaws that are making it a non-place.

Oscar Newman provides a nice example of this sort of diagnosis/tinkering, where a long city block in Brooklyn was altered to create a greater spirit of place:

> The street has been shaped to slow traffic, and symbolic portals have been located at each end. A portion of the central area of the street has been completely closed to traffic and has been turned into a play and communal area. Residents claim that street crime has been almost eliminated, that their residences are burglarized much less frequently, and that drug addicts noticeably avoid the area. On their own initiative, residents have begun to plant gardens and define the areas immediately adjacent to their houses.
>
> (Oscar Newman, *Defensible Space*)

In this instance an important design dimension was closure or enclosure, which turned a city block that was anywhere or nowhere into a concentrated activity space that was a definite somewhere for the residents. Other possibilities include encouragement of social contact (good seating, centrally located spaces), lighting (sometimes too bright, sometimes too dim, or too fixed), visibility of people to one another, and alternative activity facilities such as game areas or work spaces.

An extreme example of diagnosis/tinkering is the work of the Microweather group at Massachusetts Institute of Technology. Their work is aimed at reorganizing natural and man-made features of a farm, such as hedgerows, trees, and locations of buildings, to change the pattern of temperatures, winds,

Making a place out of the dead-end wall of a supermarket building: instant streetscape.

and sun exposure on that site. They are trying to understand the interlocking ecology of relatively small areas, to be able to influence the system in relatively productive ways—a very different effort from the typical American high-technology approach to altering settings by moving around earth, streams, buildings, and so forth, with little understanding and even less caring that all the relationships make a difference.

Not Unmaking Places

The last example implies that we also can help to provide good experiences by not unmaking places that already have a strong spirit.

During John Hillaby's walk through Europe, he found a particularly devastating example of place unmaking in a once lovely valley in the French Alps:

> What I have to say about Val d'Isere is tinged with knowledge of the disaster that happened there months later. The hillside collapsed. A landslide rolled down on the school and eighty children were buried alive. You could argue it was predictable. Trees were being uprooted with steel hawsers that afternoon (when I passed through). They were dredging the river for sand and gravel. The water flows fast and muddy and in flood it bites deep into the loose clays. But all this, I say, is being written with hindsight. My first impression was of violence. Pollution is violence and environmental pollution is environmental violence. From the gaping holes in the bare ground, it looked as if a stick of bombs had fallen across the floor of the valley. Tower cranes wind among dozens of chalets and half-completed hotels. A little army of workmen were building the Super Ski-ville of the Tarentaise.
>
> (John Hillaby, *Journey Through Europe*)

The efforts of historic preservationists have been toward not pulling down those one-of-a-kind settings that can never be duplicated or experienced again, as they were special products of a particular time and set of forces. Sometimes preservationists are successful, more often they are not.[11]

Besides preserving buildings and other historic man-made settings, there is today a strong concern with preserving wilderness areas and other natural beauty (such as the Val d'Isere). Wilderness advocates argue (and rightly, I think) that unless the forces toward continual development are counter-balanced, there will soon be no alternatives left for those who prefer natural un-developed settings. These alternatives include areas that have no roads and are therefore not overrun with people and vehicles; areas that have been somewhat developed such as national parks, but which still provide a variety of outdoor activities that cannot be done in the city or suburbs; and areas that have special qualities that can be experienced nowhere else, such as the Grand Canyon or the Florida Everglades. When an area of this last type is permanently altered, it is as if another animal species has become extinct, never to be seen again. My hope is that we will all learn to be more aware of our own habits in using special settings, and of what we can do to help keep them from becoming extinct.

HIGH-LEVERAGE SETTINGS

At the beginning of this chapter I said it would illustrate some ways of thinking about making settings with a special spirit of place. I do hope, however, that the ideas suggest other possibilities for readers to play a role in making places. The important effects are cumulative: we influence our own settings best by influencing whole patterns of design, use, and alteration, so that the impact over time is enhanced.

The other way of influencing patterns of experiences is for us to pay special attention to high-leverage settings that are used by many people, often under specific circumstances. When these settings are dull or inappropriate, they provide poor place experiences for a great many users.

Temporary Settings   Even though construction sites do not last for long (except in special cases of deliberate delay), temporary sites are facts of life for the city dweller; changing the pattern of how they are managed would therefore have a large cumulative impact. The Swiss take much more care with this process than do English or American builders, and they construct special screens for in-process buildings. In the United States, at least some construction sites have holes in the walls to allow "sidewalk superintendents" a view of the project.

Major Roadways   Because the automobile is so central to our lives today, we spend a lot of time on roadways. The more we can design them as special places, the better our cumulative experience will be.

Transport Systems   A similar argument holds for mass transit systems. They are usually settings to be gone through as quickly as possible. We could do much more with making them high-quality place experiences in themselves, such as the graduate courses given on the Long Island commuter rail line, or artworks displayed in some of the Boston MBTA stations.

Schools In the United States these settings are used by a high percentage of people in one way or another. They sometimes have a special spirit of place, but often this is in spite of design or official policy, not because of it. Edward Hyams has suggested that we should look at new schools and universities for models of how to create places with a strong human spirit, as these have been done much better than the "new towns" that have been developed in the last thirty years.[2]

Hospitals When patients and staff use a hospital, there is a heavy emphasis on task functionality—if it does not serve its medical purpose, it has failed as an institution. Yet for both patients and staff, the lack of attention to other features means that the cumulative effect may be dispiriting, even while it is supposed to be physically healing. A big difference would be made by special attention to these settings.

MAKING PERSONAL PLACES

This chapter will close with a discussion of some of the most familiar methods of making personal places that have a strong sense of identity with the owners or users, and therefore exude a special air as being different from other settings.

Marking

The simplest means for creating a personal place is simply to mark an area off as a space that is yours. Plains Indians and other nomadic tribes traditionally created personal places simply by throwing down rugs, blankets, and hides to show that the bit of ground had been claimed by a person until he chose to move his markers. Office workers mark their desks or shelves with family pictures, posters, plants, filing cabinets, and the like.

This mural made a Cambridge firehouse much more personally identified with its occupants.

Of course, the effectiveness of doing this depends on the extent to which there are norms that say that people should respect the markers. Research in a university library found that the markers used, such as a pile of books, must be part of a recognized signal language; other people must share the concept that markers should be respected; and markers are more effective if one's neighbors will enforce their messages in one's absence.[12]

The other type of marking is the unplanned trace left by intensive use. People imprint personal sections simply by the things they do as they use them. Notes on a wall, doodles on a table top, patterns of wear on stairs, colors of walls, spatters on a kitchen floor all become part of the history of life for particular people in a particular area.

Structuring

On a larger scale, we make personal places for families (and for individual family members) by the way we choose locations, houses, and arrangements within them. A striking example is Sissinghurst Castle, the home created by Harold Nicolson and Victoria Sackville-West (described by their son, Nigel):

> They repaired the surviving buildings, making two bedrooms for themselves in one of the cottages, one for Ben and me in another (which we shared until we were both at Oxford), and most important of all separate sitting rooms for each of us. There were no guest-rooms, deliberately and only one common sitting room, a room like Long Barn's, fifty feet long, which we used only occasionally. They had achieved by the accident of the physical separation of the buildings the perfect solution to our communal lives. Each of us could be alone most of the day, and we could unite for meals.
>
> (Nigel Nicolson, *Portrait of a Marriage*)

This pattern is often mirrored in larger modern American homes by the creation of adults' and children's areas that are separated and linked by common rooms.

Creating Supportive Conditions

Another strategy is concerned not with making places directly, but with creating conditions that help others imbue personal places with their identities. For instance, work organizations often allow or help members (usually their "creative types," such as researchers or advertising specialists) to shape personal areas. Unfortunately, the system, through overcontrol of facilities, blocks others in the organization from doing the same for themselves. There are cases of managers ordering the walls in an office building to be stripped of all posters, pictures, and other uncontrolled personal traces before important visitors arrived, as if it would give the company a bad name to project an image of having actual people working in its otherwise totally efficient spaces. This is not the way to create a supportive climate for making and enjoying personal places.

Some designers attempt to establish settings in overall concept, but leave some slack so that the users themselves can make decisions (such as how to divide spaces, where to place furniture, what colors to use on walls, or what artifacts to bring) that express their own personalities and work styles. I hope we will see much more of this design strategy in the future.

For low-income housing, it has been suggested that a special effort needs to be made by housing administrators to encourage personalization by residents. The goal is to encourage symbolic messages in housing that residents can identify with, and that will reinforce a positive self-image rather than the negative one associated with many housing projects.[13]

Resources for Making Personal Places

The amount of resources at one's disposal obviously has an effect on what can be done to make a personal place. Wealthy people have a wide range of choices available that are closed to the middle and lower economic groups. For example, when Mrs. E. P. Hutton was asked to sell her New York town house to a developer, she was able to strike a bargain whereby the developer recreated her 54-room mansion at the top of the new apartment house built on that site.[14]

Another way in which people of means create personal places is by collecting things that express their tastes or interests, such as art or furniture. A perfect case is the London home of Sir John Soane, a nineteenth century English architect who created a personal home/museum filled with art and other designed objects. It is preserved today and open to visitors, who are often overwhelmed by its strength as a personal place:

> The building is a curiosity of such enduring strangeness, with passages of such imaginative fancy, that one feels oddly as if one might have dreamed the whole thing. But who could dream a monk's parlor and crypt and sepulchral chamber on the basement level, a passage of classical columns on the ground floor holding aloft a wall-less mezzanine drafting room, light shafting down from lateral skylights, a miniaturized dome over an open circular well surrounded by arched passages at two levels, every surface covered with fragments of antiquities and sculptural and architectural memorabilia overflowing in a monument court and a monk's yard and tomb?

> (Ada Louise Huxtable, "The Curiously Contemporary Case of Sir John Soane," *New York Times*, November 24, 1968)

Soane created a strong spirit of place both through collecting and through structuring the background setting in special ways to fit his sense of self. This is undoubtedly easier for architects than for most other people, as they can work directly with the form of their setting and usually have the technical knowledge to shape it themselves. The result is often a more immediate, personal statement. Thus many office experiments are worked out by designers first in their own work places and then applied elsewhere.

Physical and social change combined: overcoming social norms to make a usable family space out of the front lawn.

For those who have few economic resources, it is not impossible to create personal places, but it does require different strategies. In the home, anyone can shape a territory through identifying certain space or furniture as one's own, or by filling some spot with simple objects of special meaning. Families who cannot afford elaborate private facilities define the public areas surrounding their home as part of their personal place. The social life in low-income neighborhoods revolves around the steps, stoops, and streets, which become extensions of the apartments. It is sometimes hard to tell where the inside leaves off and the outside begins.[15]

The Scale of Personal Places

This discussion has considered personal places of a fairly moderate size, from a space within a home or office to a building and its surroundings. The size of personal places can run all the way from very small (one's body space, or "personal space bubble," as it is called) to quite large (towns, regions, or countries). On the larger end, Gilbert White's personal place, as revealed in his letters on *The Natural History of Selborne*, was not limited to his house. It included the whole Hampshire town of Selborne and its neighborhood, which to this day bear his stamp in their atmosphere.

The Amish created an unmistakeable personal place in the Lancaster, Pennsylvania area through their distinctive buildings, carriages, and overall life style. More recently, the new town of Columbia, Maryland bears the strong imprint of its developer and prime mover, James Rouse. It is a setting that reflects his energy, values, and commitment to the long-term creation of quality environment. This reminds me of the spirit of the English landowners of the eighteenth and nineteenth centuries who created great personal land-

IMPROVING OUR SENSE OF PLACE

scape parks that they would not see completed in their lifetimes. They literally invested in places that could only be fully enjoyed by future generations. Except for efforts such as Rouse's, the tendency today is to try to create instant places, such as by buying full-grown trees from nurseries. This is not a bad choice if you start with a bare site, but it does not look very far toward creating a future setting that cannot be finished instantly.

I should add a note here about rigged personal places. These are sites established as memorials to people after they have died. This works well if the site was indeed a personal place (such as Darwin's Down House, or Soane's house in London) so that it seems still to have real traces of the individual. It falls flat, however, when the setting is manufactured with memorabilia that were never together when the person was alive, such as London's Old Curiosity Shop, which is supposed to evoke the aura of Dickens, but just comes off as a tourist trap.

MAKING PLACES

At this point we can return to the question that started off this chapter: can places be made? I think that the points and examples provided suggest that the answer be a qualified yes. We can shape settings so that they will have a strong spirit of place through their sharp identity, human vitality, rich symbolic messages that stimulate fantasies and memories, structures that shape people's experiences in certain patterns or sequences, and special opportunities. We can also make place experiences by shaping ourselves in certain settings: finding out in advance about the history or features of a new setting, looking for features, clearing ourselves and focusing on the present, and allowing ourselves to free-associate with the sights, sounds, and smells in the setting.

Finally, while not many of us are ever in the position of having the power to create or shape whole towns, we do have some potentially potent options. For one, we can be a force for not unmaking places, by helping to preserve settings with a special spirit of place, whether they are urban, suburban, or rural. We can buck the trend toward standardization and homogenization of settings into indistinguishable strips of office blocks, hotels, gas stations, and fast-food outlets. Our other great potential is in the creation of personal places: having the interest, concern, and curiosity to put our own special stamp on some spot, so that we and others know that a bit of ourselves emerges and enlivens a real place in the world.

NOTES

1. Geoffrey and Susan Jellicoe, *The Landscape of Man*, New York: The Viking Press, 1975.
2. For some examples, see Bernard Rudofsky, *Streets for People* (Garden City, N.Y.: Doubleday, 1969); Gordon Cullen, *The Concise Townscape* (London: *The Archi-*

tectural Press, 1961); Constance Perin, *With Man in Mind* (Cambridge, Mass. and London: The MIT Press, 1970); E. Relph, *Place and Placelessness* (London: Pion Ltd., 1976); and Edward Hyams, *The Changing Face of England*, (London; Kestrel Books, 1974, Paladin Edition as *The Changing Face of Britain*, 1977).

3. Mark Girouard, *The Victorian Country House*, New Haven: Yale University Press, 1979, p. 216.

4. For a very interesting treatment of the design problems of successful connected growth, see Brent C. Brolin, *Architecture in Context: Fitting New Buildings With Old* (New York: Van Nostrand Reinhold, 1980).

5. Francis Duffy, "Office Building: The Place and the Process," *The Architects' Journal*, May, 1973, pp. 1063–1067.

6. See Colin Turnbull, *The Mountain People* (New York: Simon & Schuster 1972, p. 27).

7. Norman Ashcraft and Albert Scheflen, *People Space: The Making and Breaking of Boundaries*, Garden City, N.Y.: Anchor Books, 1976, p. 41.

8. Kevin Lynch, *What Time Is This Place?*, Cambridge, Mass. and London: The MIT Press, 1972.

9. For a practical description of the reuse of old buildings such as churches, warehouses, barns, and schools, see Jean and Cle Kinney, *47 Creative Homes That Started as Bargain Buildings* (New York: Funk & Wagnalls, 1974).

10. See Ada Louise Huxtable, "The Fall and Rise of Main Street," *New York Times Magazine*, May 30, 1976, pp. 12–14.

11. For a sad catalogue of the failures, see Hermione Hobhouse, *Lost London* (Boston: Houghton Mifflin, 1972) and a companion volume, *Lost New York*, by Nathan Silver.

12. Robert Sommer, *Personal Space: The Behavioral Basis of Design*, Englewood Cliffs, N.J.: Prentice-Hall, 1969, Chapters 3 through 5.

13. Franklin D. Becker, *Housing Messages*, Stroudsburg, Pa.: Dowden, Hutchinson and Ross, Inc., 1977, Chapter 4.

14. Andrew Alpern, *Apartments for the Affluent*, New York: McGraw-Hill Book Co., 1975, p. 108.

15. Interestingly, eighteenth century landscape architect Humphrey Repton used the same strategy in creating his personal living place. He experimented with what he called "appropriating" the public road as part of his own garden area. See David Jarett, *The English Landscape Garden* (New York: Rizzoli, 1978, p. 144).

19 Making Sense of Place

I have referred throughout this book to phrases such as the place experience, micro-world experiences, rich experiences with settings, so on. The word experience has recurred for a specific reason: I see our experiences as the only things we can really "have" or own as persons. It is the one commodity that belongs to us and no one else, and cannot be destroyed by fire, theft, or next year's trend in fashions. I have therefore focused on having rich place experiences as one of the major gains from having good interactions with our settings. This consequence contrasts with other obvious ones that are valued in Western industrial society, such as accumulating a lot of physical things, or "punching tickets" (gaining social status by having visited the accepted sites of the well-traveled person).

In the long run, we enrich our lives most when we focus on enriching our experiences rather than simply maximizing our things or our excursions. Thus there have been several instances in this book where a richer place experience is predicted from having fewer possessions, not more (such as freeing oneself from encumbering equipment in order to concentrate on the setting), or from visiting only one national park on a vacation, not several.

One implication is that we should value our own experiences as they are, not as they "should" be on some conventional scale. This acceptance can make the most difference at moments when we have a choice about how to orient ourselves to our setting, which in turn controls how we will see, use, and experience that setting.

Imagine for a moment that you are driving from Boston to Montreal and your car breaks down temporarily in Brattleboro, Vermont. Once you have your car in the hands of a competent mechanic, you have a choice to make. You can assume that the time it takes to repair the car is lost or dead time, simply a space to be filled until you can get back on to your original planned track, or you can take it as a gift of an unstructured period to explore a new setting, and wander around to see the various sides of Brattleboro. If you take the former approach your memories of Brattleboro will be mainly flashes of feelings of anger, while if you take the surprise opportunity the experiences and memories are quite unpredictable, but likely to be both more interesting and more fun.

In order to take this situation as an opportunity, you have to choose to clear yourself and let go of your righteous anger at being let down by your vehicle, or your anxiety at not sticking to your original travel schedule, and then start fresh in the present, using where you are at the moment as what you have to work with. It is obviously your best way of salvaging the potential experience, and it can often be much better than just a salvage operation, especially in places that you would never have thought to spend time. I have known instances of new life-long interests being formed by just such a chance event, when people let go of their sense of injustice and allowed their curiosity to become the guiding force in choosing what to do with their time in a setting.

I hope that this example (and the book as a whole) has shown that when it comes to blaming places for being no good, in some instances we should direct the blame a bit further and include our own attitudes and expectations as well. When we write off a vacation place as being too dirty, we should also examine our own inflexible standards about cleanliness, which may be unrealistic in a country setting. When we complain about a city as a cold, unfriendly place, we should include our expectations of unfriendliness that led us to avoid initiating social situations. When we believe that we "know" a particular setting, we should be aware of the fact that we are carrying a store of images that were *our* reality of the moment when we were there, but they are not necessarily descriptive of its varied features. These images are a blend of the setting and our own mood, expectations, intentions, sequences of actions, and reactions. We therefore need to keep an open mind about our own judgments and pronouncements, and acknowledge that we do not know about a location's other moods that we have not seen.

THE HIGH-QUALITY PLACE EXPERIENCE

I have tried to examine a corner of the role that experiences fill in our lives. One aspect of this examination was an implied definition of a high-quality place experience. In general, our experiences in a setting are higher-quality if we

- like being there;
- enjoy activities there;
- are stimulated to think of ourselves or the setting in new ways, with new possibilities;
- are stimulated to rich images, fantasies, memories, or feelings;
- can do those tasks we want to do, and do them well in the setting;
- can relate well to other people there;
- are not degraded or destroyed by the process of being in the setting, and do not destroy it for others;
- have a sense of being somewhere specific that has an identity and image, and do not feel we are nowhere.

The sense of place can refer not just to a person's sensation, but also to whether or not it makes sense as a place for human use. A large number of attributes of settings have been examined, and some were identified as likely to contribute to high-quality place experiences. These included: good facilities for one's activities; rich traces of history; features that give the setting a strong sense of identity or that create a mood of mystery; potent geographic characteristics that shape the lives of people; boundaries or enclosures that differentiate a setting from its surroundings; particular patterns or groupings of people who generate a certain vitality and climate; opportunities to do things that cannot be done elsewhere; and social norms that create a pleasant or stimulating social climate.

Some settings contain many of these features, while others may have relatively few of them and thus have a weak spirit of place. Others may have only one attribute (such as historical traces) that is so strong that it generates a definite spirit of place that will be experienced in a similar manner by different types of people. Still others are so lacking in distinctive features as to do a kind of violence to our sensibilities if we spend much time in them; it is literally like being suspended in a stimulation-free environment.

It should be pointed out again that one can have a quality experience from a good setting without owning it. Our range of usable places is much greater than those we own directly, which is why we should be demanding in terms of decisions that affect public spaces and facilities. We can use many nonexclusive settings such as streets, shop windows, public squares, and libraries without spending anything except the energy that it takes to pay attention to where we are and what it is like for us. Similarly, one can own a great deal of property and a variety of rich settings and get little from them in the way of place experiences, if one's stance toward them blinds one to most of their possibilities.

TYPES OF PLACE SENSE

My interest in high-quality place experiences is naturally based on the old saw that everybody must be someplace, all the time. Over time, our images of places are threads or links in the patterns of our lives. They are like a skeleton, a fabric, or a series of stages on which we develop our various roles. These place experiences can be consistent, changing, different, surprising, predictable, good, bad, stagnating, stimulating, expanding, lively, dull, and anything else that human beings are capable of feeling and thinking. Some of these reactions are conscious, while many others are not, and influence us in ways we only notice later, if at all.

The discussions in this book have been guided by the assumption that there are relatively small numbers of major characteristics of place that account for much of the richness in our relations with our settings. The main types include:

- identity
- history
- fantasy
- mystery
- joy
- surprise
- security
- vitality
- memory

We may experience a setting as having none, one, or a combination of these characteristics; this experience will also vary with our own expectations and mood, so that we are likely to notice more at some times than at others.

Some of our strongest place experiences come from seeing a new setting with fresh eyes; others, equally strong, come from the recognition of elements in a new setting about which we have acquired advance information. Some people learn to like place experiences for their own sake, finding those moments as some of the inherently interesting parts of life. These place people make choices aimed at increasing the frequency of their significant place experiences: they travel, they attempt to influence decisions about public settings, and they create high-quality areas of personal places. They may focus on getting to know one micro-world quite well, or on seeking out and exploring many varied settings, or on alternating these experiences at different times in their lives.

People who have rich place experiences use all their senses to tune in to what surrounds them more than less aware people do. They also use their internal sense—the imagination—in rich ways, generating both memories and fantasies that multiply the images and satisfactions a setting can provide.

Unfortunately, there are probably more examples of low-quality place experiences than of high-quality. This is true partly because many people do not use their senses, imaginations, or memories to use the opportunities settings provide. In many instances, they do not even give themselves a chance to see new things because they structure their activities and time patterns so that they have little leeway to let new images emerge.

Low-quality place experiences also are frequent because so many settings do not provide much in the way of interesting spirit and opportunities, being bland or degenerated, with poor encouragement to the spirit. These settings are often designed for machines or by using statistical models of efficiency, but not for the variety of its users. Others were capable of generating a strong sense of place at one time, but have been steadily degenerated by use so that they figuratively (or literally) become slag heaps fit for nothing but stimulating awareness of the fact that waste is a universal problem.

I hope that at a minimum this book may have stimulated in you a desire to obtain some new enjoyment from settings you now use. In addition, it may eventually change some patterns in how you choose and shape your settings in the future, so that opportunities are more often fulfilled. I believe that this direction can lead both to a richer individual life and to a better collective use of resources in a period of shrinking supply and expanding demand.

The sense of place is, in the end, the result of a complex mixture of physical, social, and personal factors. When this mix is poor, we have a feeling of dis-ease, of being out of place, that can be very discomfiting. This condition is worth recognizing, so that we can change the mix of place factors sooner rather than later, acting for ourselves, rather than waiting for things to change. In order to do this, we have to assume that our own choices affect the mix, rather than thinking that it is just the world's random forces at work. Fate helps to make our experiences; so do we, by the choices we make, the attitudes we assume, and the extent to which we seek quality place experiences for ourselves and promote them for others.

Bibliography

Abbey, Edward, *Desert Solitaire: A Season in the Wilderness* (New York: McGraw-Hill Book Co., 1968).

Abramovitz, Anita, *People and Spaces: A View of History through Architecture* (New York: The Viking Press, 1979).

Alpern, Andrew, *Apartments for the Affluent* (New York: McGraw-Hill Book Co., 1975).

Ashcraft, Norman and Albert Scheflen, *People Space* (Garden City, N.Y.: Anchor Doubleday 1976).

Bachelard, Gaston, *The Poetics of Space* (Paris: Presses Universitaires de France, 1958) (Boston: Beacon Press edition, 1969).

Becker, Franklin D., *Housing Messages* (Stroudsburg, Pa.: Dowden, Hutchinson & Ross, Inc., 1977).

Benchley, Nathaniel, *Robert Benchley* (New York: McGraw-Hill Book Co., 1955).

Beston, Henry, *Northern Farm* (New York: Holt, Rinehart and Winston, 1948) (Ballantine Books edition, 1972).

Blythe, Ronald, *Akenfield* (New York: Pantheon Books, 1969) (Delta edition, 1970).

Brolin, Brent C., *Architecture in Context: Fitting New Buildings with Old* (New York: Van Nostrand Reinhold, 1980).

Canter, David, *The Psychology of Place* (London: The Architectural Press, 1977).

Castaneda, Carlos, *A Separate Reality* (New York: Simon & Schuster Touchstone, 1971).

Cavett, Dick and Christopher Porterfield, *Cavett* (New York and London: Harcourt Brace Jovanovich, 1974).

Clark, Kenneth, *Another Part of the Wood* (New York: Harper & Row, 1974).

Coleman, John R., *Blue-Collar Journal: A College President's Sabbatical* (Philadelphia: J. B. Lippincott, 1974).

Cullen, Gordon, *The Concise Townscape* (London: The Architectural Press, 1961).

DeCamp, L. Sprague and Catherine C. DeCamp, *Ancient Ruins and Archaeology* (London: Souvenir Press Ltd., 1965) (Fontana edition, retitled *Citadels of Mystery*, 1972).

Drawbell, James, *Scotland Bittersweet* (London: James Macdonald & Co., Ltd., 1972).

Duhl, Leonard, *The Urban Condition: People and Policy in the Metropolis* (New York: Basic Books, 1963).

Fairbrother, Nan, *The Nature of Landscape Design* (London: The Architectural Press, 1974).

Fairbrother, Nan, *New Lives, New Landscapes* (Harmondsworth, Middlesex: Penguin Books, 1972).

Fletcher, Colin, *The Man Who Walked Through Time* (New York: Alfred A. Knopf, 1968).

Gibson, J. J., *The Senses Considered as Perceptual Systems* (Boston: Houghton-Mifflin, 1966).

Girouard, Mark, *Life in the English Country House* (New Haven: Yale University Press, 1978).

Girouard, Mark, *The Victorian Country House* (New Haven: Yale University Press, 1979).

Goffman, Erving, *Asylums* (Garden City, N.Y.: Anchor Doubleday, 1961).

Goffman, Erving, *The Presentation of Self in Everyday Life* (Garden City, N.Y.: Anchor Doubleday, 1959).

Gould, Peter and Rodney White, *Mental Maps* (Harmondsworth, Middlesex: Penguin Books, 1974).

Hadfield, Charles and Mary Hadfield, *The Cotswolds* (London: William Clowes and Sons, Ltd., 1966).

Hall, E. T., *The Hidden Dimension* (Garden City, N.Y.: Anchor Doubleday, 1966).

Hemp, William H., *New York Enclaves* (New York: Clarkson N. Potter, 1975).

Herriot, James, *All Things Bright and Beautiful* (New York: St. Martin's Press, 1973).

Herriot, James, *James Herriot's Yorkshire* (New York: St. Martin's Press, 1979).

Hillaby, John, *Journey Through Europe* (London: Constable and Co., Ltd., 1972) (Paladin edition, 1974).

Hobhouse, Hermione, *Lost London* (Boston: Houghton Mifflin, 1972).

Huxtable, Ada Louise, *Will They Ever Finish Bruckner Boulevard?* (New York: Macmillan, 1971).

Hyams, Edward, *The Changing Face of Britain* (London: Paladin, 1977).

Jacobs, Jane, *The Death and Life of Great American Cities* (New York: Vintage Books, 1961).

Jarrett, David, *The English Landscape Garden* (New York: Rizzoli, 1978).

Jasen, David, *P. G. Wodehouse: A Portrait of a Master* (New York: Mason and Lipscomb, 1974).

Jellicoe, Geoffrey and Susan Jellicoe, *The Landscape of Man* (London: Thames and Hudson, 1975).

Jourard, Sidney, *Disclosing Man to Himself* (New York: Van Nostrand, 1968).

Jourard, Sidney, *The Transparent Self* (New York: Van Nostrand, 1964).

Jung, C. G., *Memories, Dreams, Reflections* (edited by Aniela Jaffé), (New York: Vintage Books, 1963).

Kinney, Jean and Cle Kinney, *47 Creative Homes that Started as Bargain Buildings* (New York: Funk & Wagnalls, 1974).

Kitchen, Paddy, *A Most Unsettling Person* (New York: Saturday Review Press, 1975).

Lanham, Url, *The Bone Hunters* (New York: Columbia University Press, 1973).

Lessing, Doris, *The Temptation of Jack Orkney and Other Stories* (New York: Alfred A. Knopf, 1972) (Bantam edition, 1974).

Liu, Ben-Chieh, *Quality of Life Indicators in the U.S. Metropolitan Areas*, 1970 (Kansas City, Mo.: Midwest Research Institute, 1975).

Lynch, Kevin, *The Image of the City* (Cambridge, Mass.: The MIT Press, 1960).

Lynch, Kevin, *What Time Is This Place?* (Cambridge, Mass. and London: The MIT Press, 1972).

McLuhan, T. C., *Touch the Earth, A Self-Portrait of Indian Existence* (New York: Promontory Press, 1971).

Mercer, Charles, *Living in Cities: Psychology and the Urban Environment* (Harmondsworth, Middlesex: Penguin Books, 1975).

Michelson, William, *Environmental Choice, Human Behavior, and Residential Satisfaction* (New York: Oxford University Press, 1977).

Milne, Christopher, *The Enchanted Places* (London: Eyre Methuen, 1974) (Penguin edition, 1976).

Momaday, N. Scott, *House Made of Dawn* (New York: Harper & Row, 1968)(Signet edition, 1969).

Morehead, Alan, *No Room in the Ark* (New York: Harper and Bros., 1959).

Moorhouse, Geoffrey, *The Other England: Britain in the Sixties* (Harmondsworth, Middlesex: Penguin, 1964).

Morris, James, *Places* (New York: Harcourt Brace Jovanovich, 1972).

Morris, Jan, *Travels* (London and New York: Harcourt Brace Jovanovich, 1976).

Mowat, Farley, *People of the Deer* (New York: Pyramid Books, 1968).

Mumford, Lewis, *The City in History* (New York: Harcourt, Brace and World, 1961).

Newman, Oscar, *Defensible Space* (New York: Collier Books, 1973).

Nicolson, Harold, *Diaries and Letters*, Vol. 3 (ed. Nigel Nicolson) (London: William Collins Sons, Ltd., 1968).

Nicolson, Nigel, *Portrait of a Marriage* (New York: Atheneum, 1973).

Norton, Boyd, *Rivers of the Rockies* (Chicago: Rand McNally & Co., 1975).

Percy, Walker, *The Moviegoer* (New York: Alfred A. Knopf, 1961).

Perin, Constance, *With Man in Mind* (Cambridge, Mass. and London: The MIT Press, 1970).

Perls, Fritz, Ralph Hefferline, and Paul Goodman, *Gestalt Therapy* (New York: Delta, 1951).

Powell, Anthony, *The Kindly Ones* (London: William Heinemann, Ltd., 1962) (Fontana edition, 1971).

Powell, Anthony, *What's Become of Waring?* (London: Cassell, 1939) (Penguin edition, 1962).

Proshansky, Harold, William Ittelson, and Leanne Rivlin, *Environmental Psychology* (Revised edition) (New York: Holt, Rinehart and Winston, 1976).

Raistrick, Arthur, *The Pennine Dales* (London: Eyre and Spottiswoode, Ltd., 1968) (Arrow edition, 1972).

Relph, Edward, *Place and Placelessness* (London: Pion Ltd., 1976).

Rudofsky, Bernard, *Streets for People* (Garden City, N.Y.: Anchor Doubleday, 1969).

Saroyan, William, *Places Where I've Done Time* (New York: Praeger Publishers, 1972).

Scott-James, Ann, *The Making of Sissinghurst* (London: Michael Joseph Publishers, 1973).

Solzhenitsyn, Alexander, *The First Circle* (London: William Collins, 1968) (Fontana edition, 1968).

Sommer, Robert, *Personal Space: The Behavioral Basis of Design* (Englewood Cliffs, N.J.: Prentice-Hall, 1969).

Steele, F. I., *Physical Settings and Organization Development* (Reading, Mass.: Addison-Wesley Publishing Co., 1973).

Steele, F. I. and Stephen Jenks, *The Feel of the Work Place: Understanding and Improving Organizational Climate* (Reading, Mass.: Addison-Wesley Publishing Co., 1977).

Teale, Edwin Way, *Journey Into Summer* (New York: Dodd Mead & Co., 1960).

Teale, Edwin Way, *A Naturalist Buys an Old Farm* (New York: Dodd Mead & Co., 1974).

Tuan, Yi-Fu, *Space and Place: The Perspective of Experience* (Minneapolis: University of Minnesota Press, 1977).

Tuan, Yi-Fu, *Topophilia: A Study of Environmental Perception, Attitudes, and Values* (Englewood Cliffs, N.J.: Prentice-Hall, 1974).

Turnbull, Colin, *The Mountain People* (New York: Simon & Schuster, 1972).

Waters, Frank, *Pumpkin Seed Point* (Chicago: Swallow Press, 1969).

Waugh, Evelyn, *Brideshead Revisited* (London: Chapman and Hall, 1945) (Penguin edition, 1951).

Winks, Robin, *The Historian as Detective* (New York: Harper Colophon, 1970).

Wodehouse, P. G. *Author! Author!* (New York: Simon & Schuster, 1962).

Wodehouse, P. G., *Leave it to Psmith* (London: Beagle Books, 1923) (Penguin edition, 1971).

Index